THE
POWER
OF
PRAYER
AND THE
PROMISED
LAND

THE POTENTIAL OF AMERICA'S REFUGEE
RESETTLEMENT PROGRAM

DR. JOSEPH BOOMENYO

iUniverse

THE POWER OF PRAYER AND THE PROMISED LAND
THE POTENTIAL OF AMERICA'S REFUGEE RESETTLEMENT PROGRAM

iUniverse books may be ordered through booksellers or by contacting:

iUniverse
1663 Liberty Drive
Bloomington, IN 47403
www.iuniverse.com
844-349-9409

Because of the dynamic nature of the Internet, any web addresses or links contained in this book may have changed since publication and may no longer be valid. The views expressed in this work are solely those of the author and do not necessarily reflect the views of the publisher, and the publisher hereby disclaims any responsibility for them.

Any people depicted in stock imagery provided by Getty Images are models, and such images are being used for illustrative purposes only.
Certain stock imagery © Getty Images.

ISBN: 978-1-6632-2481-1 (sc)
ISBN: 978-1-6632-2482-8 (e)

Library of Congress Control Number: 2021923713

Print information available on the last page.

iUniverse rev. date: 11/19/2021

DEDICATION

To my father, Rev. Mnyaci Wilondja, who went to be with the Lord on July 18, 2013. His legacy of love, unity, servitude, and sacrificial leadership will always be remembered. He was a loving father and close friend. May his soul rest in eternal peace.

CONTENTS

ACKNOWLEDGEMENT

The writing of this book would not have been possible without the help of God. I am grateful to Him. Also, I extend my gratitude to my wife, children, and extended family and to church members for prayer and encouragement.

I am grateful to my senior pastor J. Daniel Smith for the encouragement and support. I thank Madam Sue Vaughn, Karen Morrow, Barbra Alvarez, and Mr. Jean-Marie Ebulela for proofreading. Thanks to all the people who participated and contributed in different ways.

FOREWORD

I recently attended a celebration reception event to mark an anniversary of a friend of mine. While mingling with the guests in the room, a kind lady greeted me, whereupon we began a conversation about her family and her life journey. Quickly into the conversation, she asked, "May I tell you my story?" With my response in the affirmative, she told me the story of her life, which obviously held great significance for her. I left that conversation being reminded how important it is to know your story, give great value to your story, and always be ready to share your story. Your story is important, for in it lies the testimony of the grace of God upon your life.

Dr. Joseph Boomenyo has a story to share with you. It is not only an important story, but it is also an extremely inspiring, motivational, and faith-building tale. While the details of his story might be unique to him, the principles he shares on prayer, trusting in God, and basing your faith on the incomparable Word of God are those that can apply to all of us. As you read his story, I am confident, it will encourage you to lift up a quiet prayer to Jesus, asking His continued grace upon your life as your story continues to be written.

Dr. Boomenyo is more to me than simply the fine author of this book. He is a dearly trusted friend. He is a partner in ministry, as we are yoked together in the work of advancing the Kingdom of God. Our years in service together have allowed me to see closely what a man of integrity he is, as well as the magnitude of his impeccable character. Thus, I am blessed and highly favored to participate in the journey of his story. Though there are many more pages to be written in the story of his life, please allow these pages to point you to the power of the resurrected Christ and begin to have your vision enlarged for what God can do with, for, and through you for the glory of His excellent name.

Pastor J. Daniel Smith
Bethesda Community Church
Fort Worth, TX

INTRODUCTION

Every life is packaged with stories worth telling, and no one else can tell them better than the person who lived them. You are reading a book written by a person who has been forced to leave his country of origin and habitual residence due to a civil war and lived in a country of asylum as a refugee for twenty years. This man has experienced and seen with his own eyes the misery, vulnerability, and plight of refugees living in various refugee camps in African countries. He decided to sacrificially invest his time, spiritual gifts, talents, knowledge, and abilities to contribute to the empowerment of his fellow refugees and other vulnerable people in communities through capacity building.

There are over 80 million people of concern to the United Nations High Commissioner for Refugees (UNHCR). About 30 million are refugees, and others are asylum seekers, internally displaced people, and the stateless. The message covered in this book aims to contribute to the promotion of the responsibility to respect and protect human life and to the restoration of human dignity, peace, and security and economic and human development built on a strong belief system. It will add new information to the existing body of knowledge and calls for collective action, solidarity, and strong partnership in addressing the plight of refugees around the world.

My undergraduate degree studies in rural and urban planning at the University of Zimbabwe in the City of Harare were sponsored by the United Nations High Commissioner for Refugees through DAFI (Albert Einstein German Academic Refugee Initiative) Scholarships Program. I moved further with my studies and earned a Master of Arts degree in leadership and management at the University of Zimbabwe in 2012, an Executive Master's degree in peace and governance at Africa University in 2014, and a Doctoral degree of theology in ministry at Texas University of Theology in 2021.

The Power of Prayer and the Promised Land is written to demonstrate the power of prayer and how the United States Refugee Resettlement Program is viewed by most refugees as an answered prayer to their plight. Prayer is the most indispensable and unexploited resource available and accessible to human beings for free. Prayer can bring healing to any sicknesses and diseases, resuscitate the dead, and bring salvation and a durable solution to any problems. Prayer brings positive transformation of men and women, boys and girls, and leaders and servants who faithfully and truthfully run to God in prayer with a humble heart and an attitude of confession and repentance of sins.

This book gives a particular reference to the prophet Elijah's prayer recorded in the book of James 5:16–18. The Bible says, "Therefore, confess your sins to each other and pray for each other so that you may be healed. The prayer of a righteous person is powerful and effective. Elijah was a human being, even as we are. He prayed earnestly that it would not rain, and it did not rain on the land for three and a half years. Again, he prayed, and the heavens gave rain, and the earth produced its crops." It gives comparative evidence on the living conditions and status of refugees before and after their resettlement to the United States and reveals that the United States is the "promised land" for refugees.

The Power of Prayer and the Promised Land is divided into two sections. The first section is from my personal teaching presented to Texas University of Theology for the partial fulfillment of the requirements for doctoral degree of theology in ministry. Based on my teaching, I define prayer as the place where we interact with God. It is one of the most effective and important ways of communicating with God our Father in the name of Jesus Christ, our Lord and Savior. It does not matter whether everything is going well for us or we are experiencing hardships, whether we are sick or are in good health, poor or rich, in need or in plenty; what we always need is to truly communicate with God through prayer, because only genuine prayers can be heard by God. "Prayer is not a religious form without power. It is effective and accurate and brings results" (Copeland 2020).

God can communicate to human being in different ways, but He favors us most if we communicate with Him in prayer, for the scriptures says, "Do not be anxious about anything, but in every situation, by prayer and petition, with thanksgiving, present your requests to God. And the peace of God, which transcends all understanding, will guard your hearts and your minds in Christ Jesus" (Philippians 4:6–7). The Lord is near to all who genuinely call on His name in prayer. The prayer of a righteous person can accomplish much.

Prayer is the foundation of Christian principles. For instance, Jesus Christ began His ministry on earth with prayer (Mark 1:12–13). He ended his earthly ministry with prayer (Hebrews 5:7; Matthew 26:39). He is at the right hand of God the Father interceding for us (Romans 8:34).

In *The Power of Prayer and the Promised Land*, I have given the historical background of the book of James and its original audience, purpose, major divisions, and practical application with particular focus on my personal life, family history, and ministry experience as the church planter, pastor, international speaker, and peace ambassador, and the founder and executive director of Refugee Empowerment Network, which is a 501(c)(3) nonprofit organization operating in Fort Worth, Texas.

This book is spreading hope and good news to the world experiencing the crisis of the coronavirus pandemic. According to health specialists, COVID-19 disease is caused by a coronavirus called SARS-CoV-2. You can get COVID-19 through contact with another person who have the virus. This disease is predominantly a respiratory illness and can affect other organs of the human body. People who've gotten COVID-19 have had different experiences, ranging from mild symptoms to severe illness. Symptoms usually appear within a period of two to fourteen days after exposure to the virus. COVID-19 has caused the death of millions of people around the world. However, the good news is that many governments and health specialists around the world are now providing different types of COVID-19 vaccines to prevent further loss of human life and protect people by producing immunity. For instance, United States health specialists have introduced Johnson & Johnson's Janssen, Moderna, and Pfizer-BioNTech COVID-19 vaccines.

Personally, I have been vaccinated and I am encouraging you and others to also get vaccinated to prevent the spread of COVID-19. Also, my organization, Refugee Empowerment Network advocates for and raises awareness that seeks to educate and encourage the refugee community in Fort Worth, Texas, and throughout the USA, as well as refugees around the world to be vaccinated on a voluntary basis.

On the other hand, many people including key church leaders and pastors are so afraid of the COVID-19 pandemic that they have developed a pessimistic approach toward illnesses and life. They are full of fear and see themselves as powerless and dead. They have lost hope and faith in the divine healing and protection that has been provided to them by our Heavenly Father for free. All they think and see is death. They spend much of their time talking and listening to negative news and stories of COVID-19 pandemic.

The bad news is that several mega and small churches that closed their doors and have not been providing quality and appropriate pastoral care during this season of COVID-19 are facing a huge blow including loss of significant number of members. Also, many believers are backsliding, and others will completely disengage themselves from the Christian faith, mainly because their leaders are not handling the crisis in the biblical way. My encouragement is that we need to change our mindsets. Let us invest our times in prayer, listening to the good news, which is the gospel; studying, meditating, and memorizing God's Word; and surrendering our lives to Him. He is our Father, Creator, and Healer Jehovah Rapha.

Let us encourage our people to voluntarily continue taking appropriate, locally, and internally approved, safe COVID-19 vaccines. But those who cannot take the vaccines should take other appropriate medications to eradicate COVID-19 pandemic.

Most importantly, we need to invest much of our time in spreading the gospel and declaring that Jesus is the Lord and providing proper pastoral care to the folks who the Lord has entrusted us to lead. He is omnipotent, omniscient, and omnipresent, and by His wounds, we are healed. This does not mean that we should not follow the guidelines provided by the government and health authorities. Most governments, especially the United States government, need to be praised for the actions they have undertaken in terms of providing vaccines and stimulus packages to save lives and financially support citizens and residents. This was made possible in the United States mainly because of the country's robust economy. Also, other governments in different countries of the world are implementing different interventions, which fit their social, technical, and professional expertism, economic realities, and belief systems. Right now, there are many people who have been fully vaccinated but are still being infected by COVID-19. All I am saying is that, while medical specialists may find medicine to prevent and treat diseases, true healing comes from God alone. Therefore, we need to trust God more than science and human beings. This is what the Lord says: "Cursed is the one who trusts in man, who draws strength from mere flesh and whose heart turns away from the Lord" (Jeremiah 17:5). Also, the Bible says, "It is better to take refuge in the Lord than to trust in humans. It is better to take refuge in the Lord than to trust in princes" (Psalm 118:8–9).

Furthermore, we need to bear in mind that we are aliens and strangers in this world. With or without COVID-19 pandemic, every human being, born of a woman, is destined to die. Therefore, we should not be terrified by COVID-19 pandemic. There are more diseases, such as cancer, diabetes, cardiovascular disease, HIV and AIDS, Ebola, arthritis, asthma, cystic fibrosis, and malaria; people are dying of all these diseases, and others are killed in accidents. Also, millions of people are dying every year because of social illnesses, such as poverty, hunger, malnutrition, and wars, but there has been little attention, media coverage, and political commitment in addressing these social issues that have killed more people than COVID-19 pandemic. Death is the destiny for every human being. However, there is eternal hope and gain for those who die in Christ.

I am calling the body of Christ and world leaders to continue crying to God-Jehovah Rapha for intervention through prayer, fasting, and thanksgiving. God may be testing our faith even in time of sickness. In most cases, we do not know when we are being tested. Hence, we should be more mindful of the fact that we are being watched by men, angels, and the Lord Himself. All the pain, trouble, and adversity will end with a double portion and eternal honor for those who continue to put their trust in God. Let us wake up and call on His name.

We need to thank God in prayer during difficult times; sing hymns; and trust Him for protection, healing, and victories. Paul and Silas were human beings like us. They prayed and sang in prison, and God delivered them. The same God is intervening in our situation right now. We must believe Him and pray in the name of Jesus Christ. If we confess our sins to one another and pray for each other, we will be healed, and our land will be healed (2 Chronicles 7:14). This section concludes by providing models of prayer, personal life, and ministry testimony of answered prayers.

The second section of this book focuses on the plight of refugees. There are more than 80 million people of concern to the UNHCR, and about 30 million of them are refugees.

The Power of Prayer and the Promised Land explains the difficult living conditions experienced by most refugee youth living in Tongogara Refugee Camp in Zimbabwe and other African countries. The primary focus is on Congolese refugees who are currently unable to meet their basic human needs due to limited livelihood and educational opportunities and worsening macroeconomic challenges experienced in Zimbabwe for over two decades.

Before my relocation to the United States, I conducted a research project in the Tongogara Refugee Camp in Zimbabwe, which was submitted in partial fulfillment of the requirements for the degree of master's in peace and governance from the Institute of Peace, Leadership, and Governance of Africa University. My research results serve as the baseline for comparative evidence between the living conditions of refugees in refugee camps and their new lives after resettlement to the United States.

I have focused more on Zimbabwe because that is where I lived for twenty years as a refugee and on the Democratic Republic of Congo (DRC) because it is my country of origin. Finally, I will focus on the United States because it is now my new country. I am currently a permanent resident, and I am looking forward to becoming a US citizen through naturalization in the coming years. This book concludes that the United States is the "promised land" for refugees because of the potentials and/or possibilities available in this great country.

In biblical times, the Lord said to Abram, "Go from your country, your people and your father's household to the land I will show you. "I will make you into a great nation, and I will bless you; I will make your name great, and you will be a blessing. I will bless those who bless you, and whoever curses you I will curse; and all peoples on earth will be blessed through you" (Genesis 12:1–3).

In the above passage, we see that Abram, whose name means "exalted father," is later named Abraham, meaning "the father of multitude or many nations." He was a native of Ur in Mesopotamia and was called by God (Yahweh) to leave his native country, habitual residence, and people and journey to a new and unfamiliar land, where he would become the founder of a new nation. God promised to (1) make him into a great nation, (2) bless him and bless all those who blessed him, (3) to curse whoever cursed him, (4) to make his name great, and (5) to make him a blessing to others. Abram obeyed God and left his country and his people. God fulfilled his promises to Abraham by providing a land full of honey and milk for him and his offspring. The land is currently known as the land of the Hebrew nation or Israel.

The context of the calling of Abram and how God instructed him to leave his country and his people and go to a new land is completely different than the case of refugees in modern times. But the application may easily connect. Consider that, from the era when the pilgrims moved to this country on November 11, 1620, after a voyage of sixty-six days up to our modern days, millions of people have moved to the United States of America as forced migrants. In other words, they are people whose, for the most part, were forced to leave their countries and habitual residence due to religious or political persecution.

In addition, when Italian explorer Christopher Columbus discovered America in 1492, he found the Native Americans, who are also known as the American Indians. According to World meter (2021) statistics, the current population of the United States of America is 333,643,650 as of Friday, November 12, 2021. Most of the ancestors or parents of these people came to the United States as refugees or immigrants. They moved to the United States in search of freedom, peace, security, and economic opportunities. This is the true evidence demonstrating that this country is the promised land for both immigrants and refugees. Immigrants and refugees have contributed a lot to making America a great and a prosperous country.

I moved to the United States with my wife and children in November 2017 through the Refugee Resettlement Program. I am particularly thankful to the United Nations High Commissioner for Refugees and the United States government, as well as the American people in general, for a long and rewarding tradition of welcoming refugees. I give much thanks to World Relief North Texas and their staff members for showing professionalism and compassion in welcoming my family to this country and for moving together with us beyond the usual three months designed for reception and placement. World Relief's mission is to empower the local church to serve the most vulnerable. World Relief is helpful.

The US Department of States (2020) report reveals that the United States was founded as a haven for people fleeing religious persecution, and time and time again, refugees have found freedom and prosperity in this land. This country is the promised land because it provides greater opportunities for hardworking and entrepreneurial refugees to meet and achieve their human needs.

I randomly interviewed some Congolese refugees living in Fort Worth, Arlington, and San Antonio, Texas, and most respondents clearly expressed that, unlike refugee camps, the United States has provided the opportunities for refugees to meet the following human needs:

Distributive justice

Distributive justice is the need for the fair allocation of resources among all members. It focuses on adopting positive measures to ensure that all policies, whether economic, social, cultural, or legal benefit all members equally. In the United States, refugees and their children are viewed as equal members of the society with needs to be met. Unlike in refugee camps, refugee children living in the United States attend free, quality elementary and high schools. Many refugee children and youths do very well with their studies. A few of them have already moved on to universities and colleges. The US government has provided scholarships, grants, and financial aid to deserving refugee youth. For example, my two sons, Obed and Kijana, started their academic studies at a local university in August. One of them is doing mechanical engineering studies, and the other one is studying political science. Access to lifelong, quality education is a cornerstone to refugee empowerment, self-esteem, self-sufficiency, and self-reliance.

Refugees, including the elderly and the sick, have access to medical aid, social security assistance, and food stamps. These kinds of services and resources are not available to refugees in the camps.

One of the Congolese ladies said:

> Before relocating to the US, I lived in Nyarugusu Refugee Camp in Tanzania for 18 years. Life in the camp was not easy and I was always sick. Every month, I was spending at least one to three weeks in hospital bed and my situation

was deteriorating. However, when I moved to the U.S in 2016, up to date I have never spent a night in hospital bed. I receive medical supply every month, and my health condition has greatly improved. This makes me believe that God has used the Refugee Resettlement Program to add more days to my life. Sometimes people die before their time due to poor living conditions and lack of quality medical services. There is a great difference between the living conditions in refugee camp and my new life here in the U.S. I thank the Lord for bringing me here. My coming here is an answered prayer and God's favor upon my life and the lives of many other refugees. (2021 interview)

Another lady told of her own experience in the camp:

Before relocating to the US, I lived in the city of Lusaka, Republic of Zambia, as an urban refugee. My husband and I managed to buy a piece of land in Lusaka, and we built a house. We also built some rooms that were used by tenants. We generated our monthly income by venturing into small businesses and by collecting monthly rentals from our tenants. When my husband died in 2009, things became so hard for me and my family. We were resettled to the US in August 2014. Although I am no longer working because of my advanced age, I thank the Lord and the US government for bringing us here. My children are working, and they hope to build a better future for themselves and their children in this country. My major challenge is the language barrier; I am not yet able to fluently speak the English language, but I need to get US citizenship. I am willing to learn English. I thank the US government for the Medicaid, social security assistance, and food stamps provided. (2021 interview)

The above testimonies are clear evidence of distributive justice through the fair allocation of resources among all members of the society, including refugees who resettled to this country through the US Refugee Resettlement Program.

Self-esteem

Many refugees lost their self-esteem due to a dependence syndrome instituted in refugee camps. In most camps, refugees are not allowed to work. As a result, they are totally dependent on humanitarian aid provided to them through UNHCR. Refugee esteem needs—in terms of achievement, status, responsibility, and reputation—are being restored through the resettlement program.

All human beings, including refugees, have big dreams and desire to achieve great things in their personal, family, and community lives. This can only be achieved in the context of favorable policies, a stable economic environment, and just practices. The United States has provided this enabling environment for refugees; many are now working and taking care of their own needs without depending on aid. For example, consider the story of a male refugee who talked about his experiences before and after resettling:

> When we were living in the refugee camp, I was totally broke and could not afford to buy anything for my wife and children because I was not working. With the hard life in the camp, I used to look down on myself. Every time when my children or my wife asked me to buy them something, I was viewing it as provocation. I was unable to help them and lived in anger, which resulted in conflict in our home. I was always feeling insecure and irresponsible because I was failing to take care of my family needs. Life in the camp could not enable me to buy a bike that cost only between US$50 and $100. I was living in deep poverty because of unemployment. However, when I relocated to the US through the Refugee Resettlement Program, I have managed to find a job that has enabled me to take care of my family's basic needs. I pay rent on a monthly basis; I buy and eat the food I need. I take my family to eat at restaurants on a regular basis. I now own two vehicles, which I never

dreamed to own when I was living in the camp. I now live at peace with my family members because my anger is gone. I can conclude that Refugee Resettlement Program restored my self-esteem. (2021 interview response)

Personal fulfillment

Personal fulfillment is the need to reach one's potential in all areas of life. For example, one refugee who serves as the leader for the Congolese refugee community in Fort Worth Texas said, "When I was in refugee camp, I always dreamed to have my own property in an urban area. When I relocated to the US, I worked hard with my wife and children, and we have managed to move from renting to the ownership of a six-bedroom house with a swimming pool in Arlington. We are managing to pay the mortgage. Although I have not yet finished paying my mortgage, I feel proud because my dream has been fulfilled. The fulfillment of my dream was made possible through the US government's Refugee Resettlement Program" (2021 Interview response).

Another couple said:

> When we were in the refugee camp in Namibia, we were confined to depend on the UNHCR assistance only. Although, we tried to engage in small income-generating activities through our own initiative, the conditions were limiting us from fulfilling our dreams. We are pleased to say that four years after our relocation to the United States through the Refugee Resettlement Program, we managed to move from renting to home ownership and we are paying the mortgage on monthly basis because we are both employed. We joyfully and proudly bring our monthly incomes in our home and family. We bought a new five-bedroom [home] in a better location in San Antonio, Texas. Unlike in refugee camp, we can take care of our own needs and make the right choices and plans for our personal lives and that of our children. Also, we are sponsoring students and send remittance to help our extended family members in Africa on regular basis. These possibilities have given us a sense of personal fulfillments. (2021 Interview response).

Cultural security

Cultural security is related to identity—the need for recognition of one's language, traditions, religion, cultural values, ideas, and concepts.

I am currently pastoring a Swahili congregation at Bethesda Community Church (BCC). BCC is a multicultural, multigenerational Bible-believing church located in Haltom City, Texas. The church is unique, and it comprise six different language services that meet for worship every Sunday in different rooms. Services are conducted in English, Burmese, French, Kirundi-Kinyarwanda, Spanish, and Swahili languages.

Our senior pastor, Daniel Smith, and his entire leadership team gave us a green light and are providing support for each group to conduct their services in their own language, Christian traditions, and values. This provides cultural security to refugees and immigrants. Most members of our African language services feel at home away from home.

The greatest joy is that, while we conduct our services in different rooms and different languages, we all serve one God in Jesus Christ's name. This makes this church unique, fast-growing, unstoppable, and relevant. The Bible says, "After this I looked, and there before me was a great multitude that no one could count, from every nation, tribe, people and language, standing before the throne and before the Lamb. They were wearing white robes and were holding palm branches in their hands. And they cried out in a loud voice: 'Salvation belongs to our God, who sits on the throne, and to the Lamb.' All the angels were standing around the throne and around the elders and the four living creatures. They fell down on their faces before the throne and worshiped God," (Revelation 7:9–11). This passage paints a beautiful picture of how believers from every nation, tribe, and language will stand before our God and His Son Jesus Christ in days to come.

The promotion of a multicultural and multigenerational church is particularly important because it is in line with the Great Commission of our Lord and Savior Jesus Christ as stated in Matthew 28:19–20.

Recently, we conducted membership class for the Swahili and French service congregants. The training provides opportunity for them to become effective members of the Bethesda Community Church.

Freedom

Freedom is the condition of having no physical, political, or civil restraints and having the capacity to exercise choice in all aspects of one's life.

Unlike refugee camps in many African countries that uphold encampment policies confining refugees and restricting their freedom of movement, US laws and policies provide conditions that ensure refugees the freedom of movement. They are able to travel anywhere within and outside of the United States. And they are allowed to live and work in any place they choose throughout the United States.

Participation

Participation is the need to be able to actively partake in and influence civil society.

Unlike in refugee camps, refugees can participate in political and civil activities, especially after obtaining US citizenship. They can vote or be elected to take up public office at different levels and capacities.

The US Constitution states:

> No Person except a natural born Citizen, or a Citizen of the United States, at the time of the Adoption of this Constitution, shall be eligible to the Office of President; neither shall any Person be eligible to hold the Office who shall not have attained to the Age of thirty-five Years, and been fourteen Years a Resident within the United States.

This provision gives naturalized refugees the ability to serve at various positions in the US government, except the office of president:

> The US Bill of Rights, provides for the freedom of religion, speech, the press, or the right of the people to assemble peaceably, and to petition the government for a redress of grievances. It also provides for the right of the people to keep and bear arms ... In all criminal prosecutions, the accused shall enjoy the right to a speedy and public trial, by an impartial jury of the State and district wherein the crime

shall have been committed; which district shall have been previously ascertained by law, and to be informed of the nature and cause of the accusation; to be confronted with the witnesses against him; to have compulsory process for obtaining witnesses in his favor; and to have the assistance of counsel for his defense.

In addition, one of the greatest things that makes this country unique is that none is above the law. The United States upholds respect for human life. Lack of respect for human life and a state of lawlessness were among the major causes that forced many people to leave their countries of origin and habitual residence and seek asylum in other countries before relocating to the United States. Most refugees admire the peace, security, political systems, and economic stability in the United States. The prayer and hope is that refugees can be resourced and equipped to continue participating to the economic, social and political development of this country and also contribute to the reconstruction of their countries of origin in the future.

Based on the above-named comparative evidence, I am lobbying the US government, the American people, and US churches to support President Joseph Biden's executive order to increase the ceiling and speed up the process of welcoming new refugees to the United States through the US Refugee Resettlement Program.

According to a 2020 report of the Department of State, the United States Refugee Resettlement Program is done through Presidential Determination. The process for Presidential Determination was established nearly four decades ago when Congress passed the Refugee Act of 1980 with strong bipartisan support. The legislation, which codified America's commitment to protecting refugees, states, "The president annually must consult with Congress to determine the maximum number of refugees that can be resettled to the US. the following fiscal year." In the face of the refugee crisis, Presidential Determination directly represents the United States' commitment and capacity to offer asylum to refugees.

The book concludes with a cry for peace without recourse to war. It appeals to our leaders around the world, to believers, and to all people to participate in the search for world peace through dialogue, negotiation, mediation, and genuine political willingness and commitment. The emphasis is on brainstorming and the use of theories and practices that favor peaceful conflict resolution and transformation. Models such as Boutros Boutros-Ghali's "An Agenda for Peace: Preventive Diplomacy, Peacemaking, and Peacekeeping" are discussed. As are multitrack diplomacy, as well as the contributions of Johan Galtung, Gandhi, Nelson Mandela, and Martin Luther Jr. to peace.

> According to transcend media service (2020), Galtung is internationally recognized as "the father of the discipline of peace and conflict studies" believes that peace can be achieved without recourse to war. He emphasized on mediation rather than war. Galtung theorized peacebuilding by calling for systems that would create sustainable peace. The peacebuilding structures required to address the root causes of conflict and support local capacity for peace management and conflict resolution. He believes that the culture of violence can be overcome through change of mindsets, and human behavior.

> Galtung (1996) scholarly article gave the beautiful distinction between 'negative peace' and 'positive peace'. Negative peace refers to the absence of violence. When, for example, a ceasefire is enacted, a negative peace will ensue. It is negative because something undesirable stopped happening, the violence stopped, the oppression ended. But positive peace is filled with positive content such as restoration of relationships, the creation of social systems that serve the needs of the whole population and the constructive resolution of conflict. Peace does not mean the total absence of any conflict. It means the absence of violence in all forms and the unfolding of conflict in a constructive way. Peace therefore exists where people are interacting non-violently and are managing their conflict positively—with respectful attention to the legitimate needs and interest of all concerned.

Other scholars, such as Nelson Mandela, Gandhi, and Martin Luther King Jr. played significant roles in promoting peace without recourse to war. For example, Nelson Mandela served as the president of South Africa from 1994 to 1999. He left a legacy of forgiveness and racial reconciliation. Martin Luther King Jr. is internationally recognized as the father of civil rights movement. His nonviolent peaceful demonstrations proved to the world that action without violence can be effective and successful. He left a legacy of racial unity between whites and blacks. It is no longer legal in the United States to segregate or discriminate anyone because of his or her skin color.

True believers should promote peace through diplomacy and genuine political willingness to end war. There is no development without peace and no peace without development. Therefore, initiatives to build sustainable peace and security need to move hand in hand with economic and human development initiatives (north-south cooperation) that are mutually beneficial. The rule of law needs to be observed. Believers, especially those in leadership, need to play a leading role in the promotion of respect for human life and restoration of human dignity around the world.

God is so pleased with us when we respect human life because we are created in His image. We are more valuable than any other resources on earth. As the preacher said in the book of Ecclesiastes, all these other resources such as money and material things are "vanity of vanities. All is vanity" (Ecclesiastes 1:2–4). We are the salt of the earth and the light of the world (Matthew 5:13–16). Let us promote peace through dialogue, negotiations, mediation, and genuine political willingness and commitment. Peace enforcement through military intervention should be used as the last resort. With this mindset and action, we can all address the predicament of refugees in a sustainable manner. Let us do our part and God will do the rest.

PART I

EXPLORING THE POWER OF PRAYER

CHAPTER 1

UNDERSTANDING PRAYER

Introduction

This section of the book reveals the power of prayer and how God answers prayers. It focuses on answered prayers with a particular reference to the prophet Elijah's prayer recorded in the book of James 5:16–18. The Bible says, "Therefore, confess your sins to each other and pray for each other so that you may be healed. The prayer of a righteous person is powerful and effective. Elijah was a human being, even as we are. He prayed earnestly that it would not rain, and it did not rain on the land for three and a half years. Again, he prayed, and the heavens gave rain, and the earth produced its crops."

Through exploring the power of prayer, we'll look at the historical background of the book of James, its original audience, purpose, major divisions, brief expository study of the text and practical application with particular focus on my personal life, family history, and ministry experience as a pastor and as the founder and executive director for Refugee Empowerment Network (REN), which is a 501(c)(3) nonprofit organization operating in Fort Worth, Texas. REN seeks to contribute to the empowerment of refugees through capacity building, with particular focus on training, education, and employment solutions.

Definition of prayer

Prayer is the place where we interact with God. It is one of the most effective and important ways of communicating with God our Father in the name of

Jesus Christ, our Lord and Savior. It does not matter whether everything is going well for us or we are experiencing hardships, whether we are sick or are in good health, poor or rich, in need or in plenty; what we always need is to truly communicate with God through prayer, because only genuine prayers can be heard by God. Prayer is dialogue and relationship building with God, and it is the most indispensable resource available to humanity for free. "Prayer is not a religious form without power. It is effective and accurate and brings results" (Copeland 2020). God can communicate to human being in different ways, but He favors us most if we communicate to Him in prayer, for the scriptures says, "Do not be anxious about anything, but in every situation, by prayer and petition, with thanksgiving, present your requests to God. And the peace of God, which transcends all understanding, will guard your hearts and your minds in Christ Jesus" (Philippians 4:6–7). The Lord is near to all who genuinely call on His name in prayer. The prayer of a righteous person can accomplish much.

Prayer is the foundation to Christian principles. For instance, Jesus Christ began His ministry on earth with prayer (Mark 1:12–13). He ended his earthly ministry with prayer (Hebrews 5:7, Matthew 26:39). He is at the right hand of God the Father, interceding for us (Romans 8:34).

It is through prayer that we obtain our salvation and forgiveness of sins. In other words, it is not possible for a person to receive the gift of salvation without prayer. The Bible states, "If you declare with your mouth, 'Jesus is Lord,' and believe in your heart that God raised him from the dead, you will be saved. For it is with your heart that you believe and are justified, and it is with your mouth that you profess your faith and are saved" (Romans 10:9–10).

It is through prayer that we build an intimate relationship with our God and experience His presence in our spiritual lives. Prayer demonstrates how much we love God because it is two people in love. A prayerless life reduces the ability of attracting God's presence and relationship in believer's life. The fulfillment of God's promises to believers is attracted through the power of prayer. It is through prayer that we can see God in action. Prayer requires faith and action.

The purpose of this teaching

The purpose of this teaching is to help us understand that God answers prayers.

The Bible says, "The prayer of a righteous person is powerful and effective. Elijah was a human being, even as we are. He prayed earnestly that it would not rain, and it did not rain on the land for three and a half years. Again, he prayed, and the heavens gave rain, and the earth produced its crops" (James 5:16–18).

About the author of the book of James

The book of James was written by the Apostle James, who is known as the earthly half-brother of our Lord and Savior Jesus Christ (see Matthew13:55, Mark 6:3). James did not believe in Jesus Christ as the Son of God until his transformation after the resurrection of Jesus Christ (see John 7:3–5, Acts 1:14, Galatians 1:19, and 1 Corinthians 15:7). He called himself "a servant of God and of the Lord Jesus Christ" (James 1:1). He accepted this title to justify how he was transformed from rejecting the lordship of Christ to accepting Him as the Son of God. James started and ended with an encouragement to pray (see James 1:5–8, 5:13–18).

Date the book of James was written

It was probably written as early as AD 45 before the first council of Jerusalem in AD 50. This book may be the oldest book of the New Testament. James was possibly killed in AD 62.

The original audience and purpose of the book of James

The book of James is addressed to the twelve tribes or Jewish messianic believers who were scattered abroad throughout the Mediterranean area. It is believed to be the most Jewish letter of the New Testament books (James 1:1).

The purpose and general characteristic of the book of James is to provide an everyday guide to the Christian life and conduct. In other words, it is the book of wisdom of the New Testament. It is filled with moral and ethical guidelines of Christian faith.

Major divisions of the book of James

Temptations build character (James 1:1–21)

James realized that Jewish believers who were scattered outside their native land of Israel were experiencing serious testing of their faith; he advised them how they must deal with temptation. He tried to encourage and spread hope among them. He revealed that God uses our trials not to harm us but to bring us blessing (James 1:3).

This reminds me of the time that I left my home country, the Democratic Republic of Congo, in 1997 due to civil war and fear of persecution. I found asylum in Harare, Republic of Zimbabwe, where I spent three months in prison after presenting myself to the immigration officers as a war victim refugee. The three months spent in Harare Remand Prison looked like a serious testing of my faith because living conditions in prison were not good. I had never been in prison in my life. This was my first time. I was never taken to court for trial, and this created serious anxiety and testing of my faith. The first month was exceedingly difficult for me; I was down and hopeless, and I questioned why God had allowed war to take place in my home country. After escaping death, I asked why God had allowed me to be kept in prison with no case and having never been taken before the court.

In my second month of life in prison, I changed my mindset. Instead of complaining to God, I started thanking Him and spending time in prayer, studying the Word of God, and ministering to other prisoners by sharing the gospel message and teaching Congolese songs of praise and worship to other prisoners. Some prisoners gave their lives to Christ when I ministered to them. I was highly motivated and encouraged because my three months at Harare Remand Prison turned from being a temptation to something that had built my character because I had developed an intimate relationship with our Lord Jesus Christ through prayer and through reading and studying God's Word and soul-winning ministry. This became a blessing, as prisoners I'd witnessed to had given their lives to Christ. I became well known during my three months being held at the remand prison.

When I came out of the prison with my two brothers, Matthew Lisase Rajabu and Mto Eweci, we were taken to a transit refugee camp in Harare. On arrival, we were presented a lot of gifts from the Muslim businesspeople, and they asked us to join their faith in exchange for charitable gifts. We thanked the Lord for enabling us to make an exceedingly difficult and unpopular decision by rejecting their charitable gifts. We kept our Christian faith, and God was faithful in providing for all our needs.

A month after our arrival at the Transit Refugee Camp at Cheviot Road in Waterfalls, Harare, Republic of Zimbabwe, God used us to plant our first

Christian church in that camp. Our main message was Romans 1:16, which says, "I am not ashamed of the gospel, because it is the power of God for the salvation of everyone who believes: first for the Jews, then to the Gentile."

A few months later, we had a huge harvest among the refugee community, including Muslims who surrendered and gave their lives to Christ. Later, the church spread beyond the refugee community. Today, most of our church members in Zimbabwe are local and are Zimbabwean citizens. We feel happy because the local people have embraced the church vision.

We have daughter churches planted in Canada, Australia, and other parts of the world. The daughter churches were planted by members and leaders who were attending our church assembly in Harare, Republic of Zimbabwe. They relocated to the above-named countries through the United Nations Refugee Resettlement Program. The church we planted in Zimbabwe is called Power of the Gospel to All Nations Ministries.

While scattering outside one's own native country leads to many temptations and discouragement, God can change the temptations and painful experiences into something positive that builds one's character. It is true that God sometimes uses and blesses His people through such experiences. Although trials may result in impatience, God gives His people grace so that His purpose will be fulfilled, and His kingdom expanded around the world for His honor and glory. Grace is a divine substance that God imparts to us when we are in need (Hebrews 4:16). If we choose to receive the grace of God, it can sustain us even in time of war, financial challenges, desperation, troubles, and sicknesses.

Our actions reflect our faith (James 1:22–27 & James 2)

James encouraged the Jewish community scattered outside the land of Israel to live out their faith. In other words, they must prove their faith by action or their daily living. They must be listeners and doers like those who look at themselves in the mirror. Their being and doing must go hand in hand. He emphasized integrity (James 1:22). James encouraged the Jewish people scattered around the world to receive the Word of God (1:21), hear it (James 1:23), put it into practice (James 1:22), and carefully examine it (James 1:25). He pointed out that the work reveals our faith and that disobedience of God's law is sin.

Meanwhile, Christianity must not show partiality or favoritism to the rich person or a person of high status in the society because it is a sin. Also, James emphasized the importance of becoming the friend of God. He gave an example of Abraham (James 2:23).

Our words reveal our faith (James 3)

James revealed the importance of controlling our tongues. Although the tongue is a small part of the body, it is powerful because it can determine the cause of human life. The message is that we must control our tongues. Let us use our tongue to spread the gospel of Jesus Christ and exalt His name. Let us speak blessing and spread hope. We should avoid cursing and sinful talking.

I remember the story of two people who were on their sickbeds at Parirenyatwa Hospital in Harare, Zimbabwe. During our lunchtime visits and prayer for the sick people, one of the patients said, "I am dying of headache." But his neighbor, who was more ill than him, had a different attitude. He just said, "I know I am sick, but I shall not die. I will live and declare the goodness of my Lord Jesus Christ." A week after our hospital visit, it was confirmed that the man who confessed, "I am dying of headache," died, whereas the other man who had confessed life with his own mouth was healed and discharged. This story demonstrates the power of the tongue. The words of our mouth can lead to life or death.

Many people are so afraid of COVID-19 pandemic that they have developed a pessimistic approach toward diseases, sicknesses, and life. They are full of fear and see themselves as powerless and dead. They have lost hope and faith in the divine healing and protection that has been provided to them by our Heavenly Father for free. All they think and see is death. They spend much of their time talking about and listening to negative news and stories of COVID-19 pandemic.

My encouragement is that we need to change our mindsets. Let's invest our time in prayer, listening, and studying God's Word more and surrender our lives to Him. He is our creator, Jehovah Rapha.

A Guardian article (February 08, 2021) entitled "Disease Experts Warn of Surge in Deaths from Covid Variants as US Lags in Tracking" gave warnings on the increase of new infections and deaths:

The warnings come as the US appears to have created a devastating winter wave of infections, which at one time saw more than 300,000 new infections and 4,000 deaths a day. Even though daily infections have more than halved from the peak, with death rates expected to drop soon also, the threat of the more infectious variants has some considering the possibility of a fresh surge. On Monday, the US surpassed 27 million confirmed coronavirus cases, with the country's death toll nearing 465,000. The well-understood variant of concern is the B117 strain, first detected in the United Kingdom. B117 is believed to be as much as 50% more transmissible and to be now circulating in the US, where 541 cases have been found in 33 states, according to the Centers for Disease Control and Prevention (CDC). Studies are still being conducted on how B117 may affect the effectiveness of the two vaccines currently authorized in the US, from Moderna and Pfizer. Another variant from South Africa, called B1351 and recently found in South Carolina, does appear to reduce vaccine efficacy. New strains can also affect the effectiveness of some of the only treatments for Covid-19 patients, including monoclonal antibodies." If the new variant makes the vaccines less effective and new variants come up, we could have a surge in the summer," said Mokdad. IHME's "rapid variant spread" model predicts total deaths could increase by 26,000 over the most likely scenario by May. Such a forecast would result in a total of more than 620,000 Covid-19 deaths by that time.

This reality and news are terrifying and frustrating everyone and may lead to hopelessness and chaos. However, I am encouraging believers and/ the church in the United States and around the world to wake up and call on our God. We must stand and cry to our God through prayer and intercession and ask God to take this plague away from us and to heal our land. The devil is a thief. "The thief comes only to steal and kill and destroy, but Jesus comes that we may have life and have it to the full" (John 10:10). None should die before their time. We need to continue crying to God-Jehovah Rapha and trusting Him. "The Lord is near to all who call on Him, to all who call on Him in truth" (Psalm 145:18). I am emphasizing that while medical specialists may find medicine to prevent and treat diseases, true healing comes from God alone. Therefore, we need to trust God more than we do science and human beings. Our prayers, together with countless and genuine efforts made by our medical specialists and governments, will succeed if we all continue to call on God in truth.

I remember a story of one of our leaders in the church I'm pastoring here in Texas, United States of America. He was diagnosed with prostate cancer. Doctors said his situation was getting worse. They, therefore, decided to conduct an operation on him. The patient was given an appointment for the surgery, and when he presented himself before the nurses on the appointment day, he was asked to change his clothes and be ready for the surgery procedure, which he did. Also, he was told that his sexual organ would no longer be functional and that he had little chance of living longer without the surgery, as the cancer had already spread to other parts of the body.

After changing his clothes, while he was in the waiting room, he cried to God in prayer and got a word from the Lord not to proceed with the surgery. When he told the nurses that he'd changed his mind and was no longer ready to proceed with the operation, they asked him why. He explained that he needed to go home and that he believed that God would take care of him. The nurses and doctors felt that the patient was out of his mind. They attempted to persuade him to change. They even asked a social worker to persuade him, but he remained firm on his decision to go back home and kept telling them that he'd received a word from the Lord, and he would trust His word for healing. He was asked to sign some documents in the presence of his doctor, who was angry and disappointed in the decision the patient had made.

However, I am happy to say that, as of this writing, more than one year has passed, and this brother is alive today and still having good times with his wife and, at the same time, taking care of his children. He and his family members are a great blessing to our church. I cannot testify as to whether the cancer was completely healed or not; all I know is that he is alive. He is working right now. He believed and trusted God's Word. His story reminds us of the case of the Apostle Paul and God's sufficient grace on him:

Paul said, "Even if I should choose to boast, I would not be a fool, because I would be speaking the truth. But I refrain, so no one will think more of me than is warranted by what I do or say, or because of these surpassingly great revelations. Therefore, in order to keep me from becoming conceited, I was given a thorn in my flesh, a messenger of Satan, to torment me. Three times I pleaded with the Lord to take it away from me. But he said to me, "My grace is sufficient for you, for my power is made perfect in weakness." Therefore, I will boast all the more gladly about my weaknesses, so that Christ's power may rest on me" (2 Corinthians 12:6–9 NIV).

Paul trusted God's sufficient grace for his physical condition, and God kept him in good health because he trusted Him. This is what the Lord says: "Cursed is the one who trusts in man, who draws strength from mere flesh and whose heart turns away from the Lord." (Jeremiah 17:5).

The Bible states, "Worship the Lord your God, and his blessing will be on your food and water. I will take away sickness from among you" (Exodus 23:25). All these passages are calling us to put our trust in our God and to serve Him. In most cases, God allows trouble and sicknesses to take place in the world for a purpose. In the end, all the troubles and sicknesses can be turned around by Him to work in our favor. In other words, God can turn the worsening health problems and political and economic challenges currently facing our world into a blessing because He loves us. God is sovereign, omniscient, and omnipotent. Therefore, we need to be cautious and wise in every word we speak and decision we make. Our words must reveal our faith if we are true believers. Whenever we try to question, undermine, and challenge God, we are putting Him down and lifting ourselves and our problems up above Him. This must be avoided. The church is in the trial phase. In Hebrews 12:5–8, the Apostle Paul encourages the believers to endure the trial. We must endure and pass the test.

The main goal of Christianity is to be transformed in the image of Christ and be pleasing to God for all eternity. I am writing this from the pastoral point of view. As a pastor or a spiritual leader, my role is to teach and encourage folks to have deep interactions with God through prayer and through hearing, reading, studying, and meditating on God's Word. Thus, I help them find solutions for their inner problems in the Bible and guide them to the right way and lead them to mature their faith in God, as well as encourage them to understand God's purpose, will, and plan for their life. Prayer and the words we speak with our mouths in faith are indispensable. In other words, a right confession is the key to winning God's favor and to being victorious.

By our own choice, we can turn difficulties into either tribulations or opportunities. The church needs to turn the tribulations and difficulties experienced in our contemporary era into opportunities that will solidify our faith and unity, produce great patience, and take away our pride and arrogance. Tribulations can increase our wisdom, and empathy or ability to comfort others, make us perfect and mature in our service to the Lord, and help us to be more dependent on Him. Also, tribulations or pressure and difficulties experienced can open opportunities to witness Christ to the lost world through the words of our mouth, attitudes, and practical actions.

Troubles are meant to be our servant, not our master. If we do not give up, we will receive double portions, namely total restoration in all aspects of our lives (physically, socially, spiritually, financially, economically, mentally, and emotionally) and eternal life. Therefore, we must control our tongues.

Submission builds faith (James 4)

Submitting to the will of God is key to building a strong faith. People fail to receive what they ask of God because they ask with wrong motives that create conflict between their selfish desires and God. God promises to positively answer prayer; however, He will not give to those who use it for selfishness or satisfying their own sinful desires instead of bringing glory to God (James 4:1–3). If our prayer focuses on doing the will and work of God, He will answer and take care of our needs.

Prayer demonstrates faith (James 5)

James encouraged the Jews scattered outside Israel to pray and trust God for answers because the prayer of a righteous person is powerful and effective. "Elijah was a human being, even as we are. He prayed earnestly that it would not rain, and it did not rain on the land for three and a half years. Again, he prayed, and the heavens gave rain, and the earth produced its crops" (James 5:17–18).

Based on the above discussions, one can say that the book of James demonstrates how powerful and effective prayer is. Truly, God answers prayers. Like Elijah in the Bible times, my personal life and ministry in the twenty-first century are very much characterized by answered prayer.

Expository Study of James 5:16–18

There are different methods of studying and teaching God's Word. The expository method of Bible study seeks to present truths, concepts, and principles that are taught by a Scripture passage. This method reveals biblical truth from its historical background, original meaning, interpretation, and application to our own situation. In other words, it seeks to explain the original meaning of the text for the listeners and apply it to their lives. The method does not impose a meaning on a passage but seeks the meaning from the words and grammar of the passage:

- In verses 14–15, James has given clear and precise guidelines for the sick.
- The elders of the church should be called to pray over the sick person.
- The elders should anoint him or her with oil.
- In ancient times, oil represented medicine.
- But medicine alone does not heal.
- True healing is obtained in the name of our Lord Jesus Christ.
- Prayer offered in faith will make the sick person well. This demonstrates the power of prayer.
- Any sins he or she may have committed are forgiven.

"Therefore" in James 5:16 is an adverb that means "hence" or "as a result" and connects with what the author has just said in the previous two verses (14 and 15). In actual sense, the first part of verse 16 is a summary of these two verses. James is dealing with two subject matters, namely sin and prayer:

- Sin must be confessed to one another.
- Prayer must be made for one another so that you may be healed.
- The word "effective" represents much or more.
- The word "power" represents capability, ability, or competence.
- A righteous person is someone whose sins were forgiven through faith in our Lord Jesus Christ. He or she is experiencing a sanctified life.
- The prayer of a righteous person is effective and powerful. A righteous person is anyone whose sins are forgiven, not only the elders.

Prophet Elijah

The name Elijah means the Lord is my God.

Elijah is revealed as an influential prophet and a miracle worker who lived in the northern kingdom of Israel during the reign of King Ahab (ninth century BC). His prophetic activities highlighted the unconditional loyalty to God required of the nation of Israel.

In 1 Kings 18, Elijah strongly defended the worship of the Hebrew God over that of the Canaanite deity Baal. God also performed many wonders through Elijah, including resurrection, bringing fire down from the sky, and entering heaven alive "by fire." Elijah is also described as the leader of the school of prophets known as "the sons of the prophets." He was a God-fearing man. Therefore, he was highly respected by the people of Israel. But Elijah was a man just like us. He prayed earnestly that it would not rain, and it did not rain on the land. When he prayed for the drought to end, God provided rain. James quoted this story from the book of 1 Kings 17 and 18.

The main lesson found in this passage is confession of sin and prayer. If we live a life of righteousness through confession and repentance of sins, this will make our prayers powerful and effective. Our prayers will be answered.

CHAPTER 2

BIBLICAL MODELS OF PRAYER AND EXAMPLES OF ANSWERED PRAYER

Introduction

Jesus Christ instructed his disciples, saying, "Ask and it will be given to you; seek and you will find; knock and the door will be opened to you" (Matthew 7:7 NIV). In this passage, Jesus Christ demonstrated the power of prayer. When we pray and ask with right motives and in the will of God, we shall receive. If we seek, we will find, and if we knock, the door of blessings will be opened.

There are specific biblical models that can be used in revealing the power of prayer. The models are described in the following sections.

Prayer is made to God

Many people make mistakes when praying. Some make their prayers to Abraham, others to Moses and the other prophets, and some to Mary. But they are totally wrong because Jesus instructed his disciples to make their prayer to God our Father who is in heaven (Matthew 6:9). Prayer must be made to God alone. We should pray for the name of God to be exalted and worshipped.

Prayer is made in the name of Jesus Christ

When praying we should pray in the name of Jesus Christ. He stands as the mediator between us and the Father. Jesus is our Lord, advocate, and intercessor.

In John 15:16, Jesus told his disciples, "You did not choose me, but I chose you and appointed you to go and bear fruit—fruit that will last. Then the Father will give you whatever you ask in my name." We must pray in the name of Jesus Christ.

Prayer requires confession and repentance of all known sins, iniquity, and transgression

"He who conceals his sins does not prosper, but whoever confesses and renounces them finds mercy" (Proverbs 28:13).

We cannot experience the power of prayer if we are not living a sanctified life. Therefore, it is important to begin our prayer with confession and ask for forgiveness from God our Father through the blood of Jesus Christ, His Son. Also, we must forgive those who have done wrong to us. For if we forgive other people when they sin against us, our heavenly Father will also forgive us. But if we do not forgive others their sins, our Father will not forgive our sins.

When Nehemiah heard about the trouble and suffering of his people in Jerusalem, he prayed and confessed his sins and the sins of his people before presenting his requests to God (Nehemiah 1:6–7). If we confess our sins, God will be faithful and merciful to forgive us and grant our requests as He did with Nehemiah. The prayer of a righteous person is powerful and effective. A righteous person is someone who thinks and does what is correct (or right) and holy. Let us all pursue righteousness, which can be obtained from God our Father through His Son Jesus Christ, who justifies us.

Prayer is made with thanksgiving

When we pray, we must thank God for the gift of life and for the good things and benefits we have gained from Him. "He forgives our sins and heals all our diseases. He redeems our life from the pit and crowns us with love and compassion. He satisfies all our desires with good things..." (Psalms 103:1–5). Even during difficult times, we can still thank God in prayer and singing. For example, the Apostle Paul and Silas were put into the inner prison and their feet fastened in the stocks. As they prayed and sang hymns to God and the prisoners listened to them, suddenly there was a great earthquake so that the foundation of the prison was shaken. And immediately all the doors were opened, and everyone's bonds were unfastened. This story is recorded in Acts 16:16–34.

I am writing this book during the time of the coronavirus (COVID-19) pandemic that has changed the world order. People are quarantined or locked down. Everyone has been forced to stay in their homes like prisoners and to practice social distancing, hand sanitizing, and wearing face masks to slow the spread of the pandemic.

Many people are spending the day in their homes in fear, complaining to God about the pandemic. Others complain against the government and health specialists. We thank the Lord because COVID-19 vaccine has been introduced, and this will bring some hope. We need to bear in mind that it is God who has given our medical specialists the wisdom to prevent and treat diseases and sicknesses, but true healing comes from God alone. Therefore, I am calling the body of Christ and world leaders to continue crying to God-Jehovah Rapha for intervention in prayer, fasting, and thanksgiving.

God may be testing our faith even in time of sicknesses. The passing or failing of our test determines our eternal position in heaven. Habitually, we do not know when we are being tested. Hence, we should be more mindful of the fact that we are being watched by both men, angels, and the Lord Himself. All the pain, trouble, and adversity will end with a double portion and eternal honor for those who will continue to put their trust in God. Let us wake up and call on His name.

We need to thank God in prayer during difficult times; sing hymns; and trust Him for protection, healing, and victories. Paul and Silas were human beings like us. They prayed and sang in prison, and God delivered them. The same God is intervening in our situation right now. We must believe Him and pray in the name of Jesus Christ. If we confess our sins to one another and pray for each other, we will be healed, and our land will be healed (2 Chronicles 7:14).

The Apostle Paul used his time in prison in Rome to pray for churches and leaders:

A) He prayed for the church at Ephesus (Ephesians 1:16–18).
B) He prayed for the Philippians church (Philippians 1:3–9).
C) He prayed for the church at Colossi (Colossians 1:9).
D) He prayed for Philemon and the church that was meeting in his home (Philemon 1:6).

Paul said, "For to me, to live is Christ and to die is gain" (Philippians 1:21). This is our eternal hope. Our citizenship is in heaven.

The need for diversified approaches in addressing the COVID-19 pandemic

While most developed countries' leaders have imposed strict measures, including lockdown and closure of businesses, and have provided stimulus packages to support people affected by COVID-19 pandemic, this approach will not work in many poor countries where most people (50 to 80%) are self-employed. Many make a living through farming and other informal business activities. Most people in poor countries have no savings. They survive on hand-to-mouth small businesses, and their governments have no economic capacity to provide relief and stimulus packages. As a result, millions of people in Africa, especially in countries such as Zimbabwe and the Democratic Republic of Congo are dying, not because of COVID-19 but because of starvation and trauma.

To avoid unnecessary loss of human lives and starvation, before his death, president of the United Republic of Tanzania John Magufuli, who died March 17, 2021, from a heart condition, had a different approach in addressing the COVID-19 pandemic. He called on all churches and other religious groups to pray. He encouraged a multifaceted approach, including the use of traditional medicine. He trusted God to protect Tanzanians and kept his country open for usual business activities. He, however, advised Tanzanians to follow all guidelines provided by local health specialists. His approach was highly criticized by most world leaders and the World Health Organization.

However, the truth is, if we are true human rights activists—people-oriented leaders, who are truly committed to reducing the world poverty, misery, and unemployment, we should recognize Magufuli's courage and embrace his approach. Our world leaders should acknowledge and celebrate the fact that people think differently and should constructively agree to disagree. This is a sign of true leadership, democracy, freedom, and rationality. There is a need to avoid a one-approach-fits-all mindset. Tanzania is a sovereign and independent state that has the right to design and implement policies that fit the context of its social and economic fabrics.

If lockdowns continue to be imposed, many children in the DRC will become illiterate. In other words, they will not be able to read, write, and count because of the continued closure of schools. Millions of school-going children in DRC rural areas have never touched a computer and do not know how to operate one. The current DRC government has no financial capacity to support online learning systems countrywide. Most rural areas have no electricity, and roads are in extremely poor conditions. The First and Second Congo Wars saw a great destruction of transportation infrastructure from which the country has not yet recovered.

Meanwhile, the Zimbabwe economy has suffered for decades; COVID-19 pandemic and imposed lockdown is disastrous and may lead to total collapse of the national economy. Ordinary people are seriously suffering, not because of the COVID-19 pandemic but because they are not allowed to go to work; they have no money to buy food to feed their own household members, and the government cannot afford to feed them. Zimbabweans are hardworking and independence minded. Over 52 percent of Zimbabwe's population are women, and a great number of them are self-employed widows and single mothers. Imposing lockdown on this group of people is unhuman, as it reduces them to the state of beggars. Many of them describe the lockdown imposed on them as the death penalty. The COVID-19 pandemic will lead to devastating socio-economic impact in Zimbabwe and many other African countries. Economic recovery in these countries, will take longer and many of them will be forced to borrow or apply for economic stimulus grants from developed countries and world leaders. Without such interventions, we are likely to lose millions of people who have been moved from self-sufficiency to beggars due to the COVID-19 pandemic. There is a need for solidarity and collective action in helping poor countries to recover economically. Also, there is a need to directly support and assist entrepreneurs at grassroot levels to recover from poverty, unemployment and suffering by providing them with start-up kits to venture in income-generating activities toward the achievement of household food and income-security.

The Bible says, "Learn to do right; seek justice. Defend the oppressed. Take up the cause of the fatherless; plead the case of the widow" (Isaiah 1:17). There is a need for government leaders, especially in Africa, to remove the blind eye on the vulnerable groups and immediately address this situation by implementing solutions that fit their own countries' social and economic contexts. The church should wake up and spend more time in prayer for our leaders and countries worldwide. Corporate prayer and fasting in agreement among all members of the body of Christ nationally and globally is needed. Also, the church should take positive action in helping the vulnerable people in our communities and around the world.

We should pray for the expansion of the kingdom of God and demonstration of His power

We have the responsibility to pray for the expansion of the kingdom of God on earth as it is in heaven. We need to pray for more souls to be won over to Christ. We must pray for evangelists, missionaries who travel around the world for the sake of spreading the gospel of Jesus Christ to unreached people and groups. We should pray for government leaders, pastors, and lay leaders. We need to pray for the entire body of Christ to wake up and be witnesses of Christ in their own homes, families, and other spheres of influence. We must pray for schools, teachers, students, and school administrators to be witnesses of our Lord and Savior Jesus Christ.

For example, "At the time of sacrifice, the prophet Elijah stepped forward and prayed: 'Lord, the God of Abraham, Isaac, and Israel, let it be known today that you are God in Israel and that I am your servant and have done all these things at your command. Answer me, Lord, answer me, so these people will know that you, Lord, are God, and that you are turning their hearts back again.' Then the fire of the Lord fell and burned up the sacrifice, the wood, the stones, and the soil, and licked up the water in the trench" (1 King 18:36–38).

When Peter was in prison, the church gathered and prayed for him, and God answered immediately (Acts 12:5). All these passages are calling us to pray for each other. The church needs to wake up and begin to pray. The prayer of the righteous man is powerful and effective.

We should pray for the will of God to prevail

The will of God is the most important thing that all should desire to prevail in their lifetime. We are in the world, but we are not of the world. We are the salt of the earth and the light of the world. Salt influences the food we eat. The light influences our daily activities. We should let our light shine in the darkness, so that, when people see our good deeds, they will glorify our Father who is in heaven.

Prayer requires fasting

Developing a Christian lifestyle of prayer and fasting is useful and powerful in personal Christian life. Fasting and prayer bring you closer to God. A Praying and fasting church is powerful and unstoppable. God releases His supernatural power when we develop a culture of prayer and fasting. Prayer and fasting result in answered prayers.

Prayer is made in faith, action, and trusting God for results

Faith is being sure of what we hope for and certain of what we do not see. This is what the ancients were commended for (Hebrews 11:1–2). Without faith, it is impossible to please God. Faithless prayer is ineffective. Powerful and effective prayer requires faith and trusting God.

I remember when I relocated to the United States with my family in November 2017, I was assigned to pastor a Swahili-speaking Congolese refugee congregation at Bethesda Community Church in Haltom City, Texas. The first thing I asked God to show me was the needs of our people and how I could best help them succeed spiritually and economically integrate into the American systems. Two things were presented to me as an answer to my prayer. The first answer was to start a Bible school to teach them the Word of God in our native language. The second answer was to start a nonprofit organization that would contribute to the empowerment of refugees through capacity building, with particular focus on education, training, and employment solutions.

I presented these two needs to my church leadership and congregation and got their immediate support, and we started the Bible and Theological training. The school we founded is called International Bible University (IBU). The mission of the IBU is to contribute to the accomplishment of the Great Commission of our Lord and Savior Jesus Christ through training, equipping and resourcing pastors, evangelists and missionaries in the United States and Africa. Right now, we are offering eighteen months of diploma level studies containing the following eleven modules: Pentateuch, Historical Books of the Old Testament, Poetical Books, Prophetical Books of the Old Testament, Gospels and Acts, Pauline Letters, Other letters and Revelations, Homiletics, Hermeneutics, Church Leadership, and Church Administration. Our vision is to register our university here in the US and in many African countries, especially, the Democratic Republic of Congo (DRC). We seek to expand this training program and offer diploma to master's degree level certificates. Lectures are conducted in English, Swahili, and French languages. We currently have two professors namely me and Dr. Marti Williams. In just one month, we had an enrollment of more than fifty local and international students. Given the struggling need for our training here and abroad, I am scheduled to conduct a mission trip to Africa and provide a one-week training that will be attended by 300 pastors, evangelists, and missionaries in December 2021. Beside the Bible and Theology program, we are planning diversify our academic programs to include other faculties such as social sciences, arts, humanities, health and medicine, engineering and applied science, agriculture, business studies and commerce, peace, security, human rights, and development studies. Please, prayerfully, consider partnering with us.

In July 2019, we successfully registered a 501(c)(3) nonprofit organization named Refugee Empowerment Network (REN). The registration process was amazingly fast because God had provided key persons such as Jeff and Charity Reeb, Mike and Michelle Roger, Hunter Faulkner, Pastor John Kim, Sue Vaughn, Bishop Victor Seraya, Melba Booker, and World Relief, to name just a few. They all assisted us in different and amazing ways. Jeff and Charity Reeb were even able to raise US$4,500, which was used to pay for the registration fee for Refugee Empowerment Network and for other related costs.

REN exists to show a generous welcome to refugees and empower them for successful and sustainable integration into their local communities. We are a registered nonprofit organization dedicated to providing practical, life-changing resources. We are champions for refugee vitality and resourcefulness in refugee camps and resettlement cities. We seek to build bridges and develop a multicultural connection between refugees, American churches, and American people.

Our vision is that refugees and vulnerable groups are empowered, independent community members.

Here are some of the achievements made within one year after the official registration of our organization:

A) *English as a second language.* Despite the negative impact of COVID-19, Refugee Empowerment Network provided free English lessons that benefited sixty-two non-English-speaking refugees in Fort Worth, Texas. Our classes are held at the Crossings 820 and Ladera Palms Apartments in Fort Worth, Texas. REN recommended four refugees who successfully completed three months of an intensive English training program. at Texas Christian University (TCU). REN's English training program is the pillar to the empowerment of refugees because it enables them to learn English and improve their language proficiency and communicate freely in the English language at their workplaces, at markets, in schools, and at any other places in the United States of America and throughout the world where English is a primary or secondary language. The knowledge of English is also a prerequisite for refugees to pass their United States naturalization test.

B) *Trauma informed community and counseling workshop for refugees.* Refugees we serve ran away from war and were officially resettled to the United States through the United States government and the United Nations Refugee Resettlement Program. It was revealed through the workshop that many refugees are experiencing trauma and serious mental health problems. Many refugees shared their stories and painful experiences of how they made their journey from their home countries to refugee camps in neighboring countries of Africa and how they finally made it to the United States. More training and counseling sessions are needed to promote positive mental health among the refugees we serve. The training was organized by REN and cofacilitated by a team of trainers from Women's Center, World Relief, and Refugee Empowerment Network.

C) *Refugee education, responsible parenting, and employment solutions.* REN is providing mentorship and coaching services to young refugees and encouraging them to excel in their studies. Some young refugees have taken education seriously and have completed high school, and others have moved on to college and university education. Also, we have provided career guidance and counseling to youth refugees, responsible parenting education for parents, and employment services.

D) *Sewing and computers and forklift operation program.* Refugee Empowerment Network received a donation of ten sewing machines and ten computers. The equipment enabled us to provide basic computer training to computer-illiterate refugees. Also, the computers were used by elementary, middle school, and high school refugee students who were taking their online courses with their respective schools. They used our computers for free when their Chromebooks supplied by their respective schools were not working properly. Five refugees successfully completed a forklift certification program and have improved their income.

REN has three distinctive focuses—education, training, and employment solutions. These three, coupled with the fear God, will help the refugees we serve be responsible citizens and independent community members.

E) *Refugee housing.* REN conducted three training workshops on housing and provided guidance and strategies that enabled some refugee families to achieve their American dream through hard work, budgeting, saving, and increasing their credit scores. To build better credit, we encouraged them to pay their credit card balance on time. Over ten refugee families successfully and proudly moved from home renting to home ownership. This is a terrific achievement. We are encouraging those who have moved into their new homes to make their house payments on time and on a regular basis. Most importantly, many of them are working and have become more self-sufficient with the potential of becoming independent community members and active Americans, world donors, and resource persons.

F) *Relief.* We have provided free food to over a thousand refugees and other Americans who have been negatively impacted by the COVID-19 pandemic. Fresh food boxes from the USDA have been provided to refugees on a weekly basis, including fresh milk, rice, cooking oil, meat, fruits, and vegetables. We distribute about five hundred boxes weekly. The monetary value of each box is about twenty dollars. We have also provided clothing and household items to refugees.

All these successes examples are evidence showing how God answers prayers, especially if we have faith and trust in Him. The prayer of a righteous person is powerful and effective.

We should intercede for others

We have people who are sick in hospital beds and in homes. War, hunger, COVID-19, and other calamities are affecting our world today. We need to intercede and ask God for solutions in prayer.

We should pray for our own needs and for our own blessings

The Bible tells us to pray for our daily bread, which represents our needs. We must pray for our physical and spiritual needs. When we pray, we should put our prayer into practice by working because God has promised to bless the work of our hands, along with our livestock and storehouses and many other things. If we just pray without working for what we have been praying for, our prayer will be useless. If we pray for a car or a new home, we must also work and raise enough income to meet our prayer needs. We need to pray for God's blessings upon our lives so that we can be a blessing to others. He blessed Abraham and expected him to be a blessing to others. If we are truly blessed and our blessing is not impacting other people's lives, our blessing is useless.

A female intercessor and writer, Heather Adams (2021), gives six ways to pray for God's blessing:

1. Prayer of blessing for your family
2. Prayer of blessing for your community
3. Prayer of blessing for your church and pastor
4. Prayer of blessing for your leaders
5. Prayer for blessing for the new day
6. Prayer of blessing for your ministry

The key is to have an abundance mindset in prayer by praying for ourselves and asking God to use us to be a blessing to others in prayer and action.

Examples of answered prayers

The Bible is full of evidence of and stories about the power of prayer.

Prayer of Nehemiah

For example, Nehemiah needed resources and the king's support in helping him to rebuild the walls of Jerusalem. God answered his prayer. Nehemiah and his people were able to rebuild the walls of Jerusalem in just fifty-two days. The God who answered Nehemiah is the same God yesterday, today, and forever. He is our Father and able to answer our prayers. Therefore, the prayer of faithful persons is powerful and effective.

How has God answered prayers in my personal, family, and ministry life?

My life is full of testimonies of answered prayers. From a young age to now, I have experienced God's healing in my body through prayer. My father was a minister of the gospel and served in pastoring ministry for sixty-one years before he went to be with the Lord. He taught us to live by faith through prayer, and that became our way of life.

In 1994, one of my elder brothers, Solomon Msafiri, who is a medical practitioner, had established his health institution (post de santé in French language) at a village called Abumbwe in the District of Fizi, South Kivu province in Democratic Republic of Congo (DRC). In that same village, there was another man who had already established his own post de santé about two miles away from where my brother established his post de santé. Six months after his establishment, he had attracted more clients than the other medical practitioner. The competition did not go well with the other medical practitioner, who felt that his medical clinic was being deserted because of the presence of my brother and his new medical clinic established in the area. He decided to invite my brother for lunch.

The two met and shared a meal together. While they were eating, the guy persuaded my brother to drink beer with him, something that our father never allowed us to touch or drink. However, my brother was persuaded by his colleague to drink the beer so that they could enjoy their time together. The colleague put poison in my brother's beer when he stepped away from the table. My brother had left his bottle open with some beer inside, and his colleague took advantage of him. When my brother had finished drinking the beer, he began to feel sick and collapsed two hours after that. When he was transferred to a referral hospital, he was declared dead five hours after his admission at the hospital.

The medical specialists revealed that the cause of my brother's death was poison, and his body was taken home because there were no mortuaries at that hospital and nearby places. When Solomon's body arrived at our home, the entire family was shocked, and everyone was in tears because of his sudden death. The message of my brother's death was sent to my father, who was at work at the church.

When my father came home, he was informed that Solomon had been poisoned while drinking beer with his colleague. My father felt that the cause of death for my brother Solomon was a shame to him and to our entire family and would tarnish his name and his pastoral ministry because he had been preaching and discouraging church members not to be involved in alcoholism. But now his own son was dead because of his involvement with alcohol, so my father went to the room where my brother's body had been laid down on the bed. My father asked all mourners seated in the room to step out, and he remained alone with the dead body in the room.

My father cried to God, saying, "My Father God, be it known today that I am your servant. I will not accept my son having died a shameful death. I have no encouraging testimony to give to mourners gathered here and those who we will join us on the burial day. I have no good testimony to give to the church and do not want my son Solomon to miss eternal life that you have granted us through your Son Jesus Christ for free. I cry to you, oh Lord, if I am truly your servant, let my son Solomon come back to life right now in Jesus Christ's name."

God listened and answered my father's petition favorably, and my brother came back to life twelve hours after he had been declared dead at the hospital.

My father, Msafiri Wilondja, went to be with the Lord on July 18, 2013, and my brother Solomon is still alive in the DRC. He was resurrected and completely healed by God. This was a miracle that demonstrated the power of prayer. Truly, God answers prayers. He can answer your prayers right now if you believe and trust Him. Unbelief is an enemy to overcoming what seems to be impossible.

When I registered for my undergraduate degree and master's degree programs at the University of Zimbabwe in Harare and at Africa University, I did not have enough money to pay for the program, but I trusted God for provision. He provided. God used me and my brother Matthew Lisase Rajabu to plant churches in Zimbabwe through the power of prayer.

I spent twenty years in Zimbabwe as a registered refugee. I did not live in the refugee camp, and I was able to take care of my family in the capital city of Harare. God was faithful. He always answered my prayers, and I have not struggled with food.

There is no free education program in Zimbabwe and many other African countries. Because of that, many parents fail to send their children to school due to poverty and unemployment. But God supplied for my family's needs; I was able to raise enough money and pay the school fees for my children and other extended family members. My youngest brother, Bahati Mnyaci, who is the last born in our family, has just completed his Bachelor of Science honors degree in business management at the Great Zimbabwe University. This boy, together with three other siblings, came under my guardianship in 2003. I was able to pay the school fees and other expenses for Bahati from elementary school through high school, including boarding fees, as well as for his university studies. All this was made possible through the power of prayer. God provided, and He is still providing.

The church I was pastoring in Harare, Zimbabwe, is in Hopley, which is a high-density area, and most of the residents live on less than two US dollars per day, which can be described as living in absolute poverty. Therefore, I did not expect any payment, but God sustained me and my family through daily supply.

We started and officially registered a nonprofit organization in Harare, Zimbabwe, that provided startup kits to widows, single mothers, other poor women, and refugees. Many of them successfully ventured in small income-generating businesses, such as sewing, poultry breeding, vegetable gardening, raising goats and keeping pigs, and buying and selling groceries. These projects enabled them to take care of their household needs and pay schools fees for their own children on a regular basis. I helped many people who needed my assistance and support and worked hand in hand with specific government ministries and local authorities responsible for community development and women's empowerment. God supported us in our pastoral and church planting efforts.

In addition, I started a Christian leadership training program that contributed to training pastors, evangelists, and missionaries. Also, I served as the Zimbabwe national director for Training Pastors International (TPI-USA) for thirteen years. My role was to organize, coordinate, and cofacilitate nonformal pastoral training institutes held throughout Zimbabwe and in neighboring countries. From 2003 to 2016, we were able to train over 1,300 pastors, evangelists, and missionaries. We worked in close collaboration with church umbrellas such as the Evangelical Fellowship of Zimbabwe. I am grateful to my wife, Aziza Boomenyo, who always has been my close partner and coworker.

We are inviting individuals, organizations, and churches in the United States and around the world to partner with us in helping to train pastors, evangelists, and missionaries and to assist in building churches and training centers, as well as undertaking community development projects for poverty alleviation, food security, and employment creation for the benefit of vulnerable people and refugees in Africa and in here in the United States. Furthermore, we are willing to partner with and facilitate American businesspeople in undertaking mutually beneficial economic and trade projects in the Democratic Republic of Congo and other African countries.

My education at Texas University of Theology (TXUT) was fifty percent supported through prayer. I always pray for people with different needs. Most of them have seen the hand of God because He answered their prayers.

In November 2019, our senior pastor Dan Smith presented us the theme of the year 2020 as a year of trusting God for more and more—more from his words, healing, protection, and provision. Our Swahili congregation believed, and trusted God for his Word spoken through his servant pastor J. Daniel Smith. When the COVID-19 pandemic started, the Swahili congregation was reminded of God's Words. I made a declaration that we would trust God for protection and healing. Today, I can testify that God has protected all our church members, and we have not lost a single member of our Swahili congregation and other African language services. Although everyone was negatively impacted by the COVID-19 pandemic, God has remained faithful. With these few words, I believe that God answers prayers, and He is faithful. We just need to pray in sanctification with the right attitude and in the will of God.

Dr. Joseph Boomenyo

Conclusion

In conclusion, I am emphasizing that prayer is the most powerful resource given to humankind for free. It is the place where we interact with God. It is the most effective and important way of communicating with God our Father in the name of Jesus Christ our Lord and Savior. The same God who answered Elijah is still answering our prayers and needs today. My personal and ministry life and examples discussed in this book are enough evidence of the power of prayer. Truthfully, God answers prayer. He is the same yesterday, today, and forevermore. Therefore, we should pray always and trust Him for answers. He is faithful.

References

Caram, Paul G. 2005. Turning the Curse into a Blessing: A Message of Triumph from the Book of Job. USA: Zion Christian Publications.

Copeland, Germaine. 2020. *Prayers That Avail Much: An Intercessor Handbook for Scriptural Prayers.* Fourth printing revised edition, Harrison House Publishers.

Delgado, John. 2019. Prayer Training Manual: How to Pray Effectively and Get Results. Printed in the USA.

Eckhardt, John. 2012. Prayer That Moves Mountains: Power of Prayers that Bring answers from Heaven. US Library of Congress.

Franklin, Jentezen. 2011. The Fasting Edge: Recover Your Passion, Recapture Your Dream, Restore Your Joy. Florida: Charisma House.

International Bible Society. 2007. The Holy Bible New International Version. Third impression published in Africa, Struick Christian Bibles.

Mears, Henrietta C. 2015. *What the Bible Is All About: An Inspiring Commentary on the Entire Bible.* Bible Handbook, revised and updated, Tyndale House Publishers, Inc.

Nelson, Thomas. 2014. *All the Names in the Bible: A to Z.* USA: Thomas Nelson.

Internet resources

Adams, Heather. 2021."God's Blessings." Bible Study Tools/ Accessed June 2021.https://www.biblestudytools.com/bible-study/topical-studies/prayers-for-gods-blessing.html/

Sung Joong Kim. 2019. Development of pastoral administrative leadership scale based on the theories of educational leadership/ accessed June 28, 2021.https://www.tandfonline.com/doi/full/10.1080/23311975.2019.1579963/

PART II

RESETTLEMENT AS AN ANSWERED PRAYER TO THE PLIGHT OF REFUGEES

CHAPTER 3

THE PLIGHT OF REFUGEES

Introduction

This section of the book focuses on the plight of refugees in the world, Africa, and Zimbabwe in particular. It explains how and why the Refugee Resettlement Program is an answered prayer and one of the three most effective and durable solutions to refugees' problems. Most notes are taken from my thesis, submitted in partial fulfillment of the requirements for the master's degree in peace and governance from the Institute of Peace, Leadership and Governance of Africa University.

Internal conflicts and civil wars often produce large refugee flows, mostly young people and children, who cross their national borders for fear of persecution, war, violence, and human rights violations. An increased number of refugees frequently brings about negative consequences for receiving nations, particularly in most African countries that experience their own internal economic and political challenges. This situation poses serious challenges to the international community and refugee-hosting countries, including Zimbabwe, in providing basic human needs for refugees. I will focus more on Zimbabwe because that is where I lived for twenty years as a refugee and on the Democratic Republic of Congo (DRC) because it is my country of origin. Finally, I will focus on the United States because it is now my new country. I am currently a permanent resident, and I am looking forward to becoming a US citizen in the coming years through naturalization.

I am particularly thankful to the United Nations High Commissioner for Refugees and the United States government, as well as the American people in general, for a long and rewarding tradition of welcoming refugees. The United States of America was founded as a haven for people fleeing religious persecution, and time and time again, refugees have found freedom and prosperity in this land.

The United States Refugee Resettlement Program is done through Presidential Determination. The process for Presidential Determination was established nearly four decades ago when Congress passed the Refugee Act of 1980 with strong bipartisan support. The legislation, which codified America's commitment to protecting refugees, states that the president annually must consult with Congress to determine the maximum number of refugees that can be resettled to the United States the following fiscal year. In the face of the refugee crisis, Presidential Determination directly represents the United States' commitment and capacity to offer asylum to refugees.

I am one of the beneficiaries of the US government's resettlement program. I relocated to the United States with my wife, Aziza, and our five children, Obed, Kijana, Joseph Jr., Mmassa, and Gloria, in November 2017. World Relief is the resettlement agency that received my family in Fort Worth, Texas.

From the day of our arrival in the United States to date, we have managed to make some significant contributions to the refugee community through the formation of Refugee Empowerment Network, which is a registered 501(c)(3) nonprofit organization. We have assisted more than one thousand refugees from over ten different countries. For example, in 2019 and 2020, we provided essential services, including lessons in English as a second language, forklift operation certification sponsorships, computer training, sewing skills, and sewing machine donations, and supplying food and other household goods. We educated and facilitated more than ten refugee families who successfully moved from renting to homeownership. We provided training on understanding the American systems and American citizenship preparation and application process. We also assisted many refugees in searching for employment and completing applications. They were able to secure jobs and are taking care of their own needs. Our goal is to help refugees achieve their American dreams by becoming self-sufficient and self-reliant.

World refugees

The world is confronted with an international refugee crisis that requires international attention and intervention.

UNHCR's 2021 report estimates that the global forced displacement exceeded 80 million in mid-2020. The report establishes that 45.7 million people are internally displaced, 26.3 million are refugees, and others are asylum seekers and internally displaced people. The UNHCR (mid-2013, 3, 7) report revealed that Pakistan, the Islamic Republic of Iran, Jordan, Lebanon, Kenya, Turkey, Chad, Ethiopia, China, and the United States of America were major refugee-hosting countries in the world, whereas Afghanistan, the Syrian Arab Republic, Somalia, Sudan, and the Democratic Republic of the Congo were the top five source countries of refugees. Together, they accounted for more than half (60 percent) of all refugees under UNHCR's responsibility worldwide.

According to the UNHCR 2021 report, presently, more than two-thirds of all refugees under UNHCR's mandate and Venezuelans displaced abroad come from just five countries (as of mid-2020). These include Syrian Arab Republic, 6.6 million; Venezuela, 3.7 million; Afghanistan, 2.7 million; South Sudan, 2.3 million; and Myanmar, 1.0 million. Turkey hosts the largest number of refugees, with 3.6 million people. Colombia is second, with 1.8 million, including Venezuelans displaced abroad, as of mid-2020. Pakistan hosts 1.4 million; Uganda, 1.4 million; and Germany, 1.1 million. Hundreds of thousands of refugees are also hosted in Kenya, Tanzania, Zambia, South Africa, Botswana, Namibia, Mozambique, and Zimbabwe.

The increased flow of refugees has put a burden on the international community, United Nations Refugee Agency, and refugee-hosting countries in providing protection and assistance, such as education, shelter, medical and health care, foods, employment, and other services to enable vulnerable refugees to meet their basic needs and find durable solutions to their plight. Access to education and sustainable livelihoods are the cornerstones for empowering people and enabling their self-reliance.

This includes conflict victims, such as refugees. In other words, training, and education for refugees, especially youths, can contribute to conflict alleviation. And lack of it may aggravate conflict. This view is supported by the United Nations Education Scientific and Cultural Organization (UNESCO) preamble to its 1945 Constitution, which states that, "Since wars begin in the minds of men, it is in the minds of men that the defenses of peace must be constructed" (UNESCO, 2015). In addition, providing access to quality education to refugees may significantly contribute to their social inclusion, and sustainable livelihoods opportunities can enable them to meaningfully contribute to the national development in any country.

Most refugees hosted in the refugee camps of many African countries, such as Tanzania, Uganda, Namibia, and Zimbabwe, are experiencing extremely hard living conditions due to limited educational and employment opportunities available in refugee camps. Therefore, the United Nations High Commissioner for Refugees and the international community have been providing humanitarian support through the Refugee Resettlement Program.

Most hardworking refugees resettled to the United States of America are grateful, happy, and healthy. They view the United States as their promised land because of the countless possibilities and economic power to absorb a massive workforce. The United States is unique, and over the years, this country has created an enabling environment through robust government policies, as well as peace and stability, enabling refugees to proactively plan for their personal lives and become independent community members. This is the "land of milk and honey" for refugees. Many of them are managing to achieve self-sufficiency and self-reliance. These possibilities are not available to refugees hosted in refugee camps in African countries.

According to the US Department of State's 2020 report, from 1980 through 2017, the United States has been one of the leading nations in welcoming refugees. The average Presidential Determination was 95,000, with an average number of yearly refugee arrivals of 85,000. In 2018 and 2019, the numbers dropped drastically. See the table below.

Table 1. Ceilings for refugee arrivals in the United States from 2010 to 2021

Year	Ceiling
2010	80,000
2011	80,000
2012	76,000
2013	70,000
2014	70,000
2015	70,000
2016	85,000
2017	53,716
2018	45,000
2019	30,000
2020	18,000
2021	62,500

Source: Refugee Processing Center, Admissions and Arrivals (2021)

However, it is historically believed that the United States of America was built by immigrants and refugees. Therefore, there is need for the US government to regain its leading position for a long and rewarding tradition of welcoming refugees, which is a blessing to both refugees and the United States as a country. The United States Refugee Resettlement Program restores hope. And it can contribute to the safety and protection of those who were forced to flee their home countries due to war, conflict, or persecution and can increase their possibilities for livelihood restoration and prosperity.

During his election campaigns, President Joseph Biden promised to restore the United States Refugee Resettlement Program by admitting 125,000 refugees in his first year in office. After his election, Mr. Biden said, "The United States has long stood as a beacon of hope for the downtrodden and the oppressed, a leader in resettling refugees in our humanitarian response." And he promised to reclaim that proud legacy for the United States of America. His words and promise have spread hope to millions of vulnerable and hopeless refugees who have been kept for decades in refugee camps of many African countries and other parts of the world without resident permits; without educational and livelihood opportunities (in their countries of asylum); and without hope of returning to their home countries because of insecurity, lawlessness, endless wars, violence, and fear of persecution. Despite their courage, perseverance, and resilience, most refugees—especially those living in refugee camps in countries such as Zimbabwe, Tanzania, Namibia, Zambia, Uganda, and Kenya—will not be able to realize their dreams. Therefore, I am advocating and lobbying for the resettlement of deserving vulnerable refugees to the United States and other developed countries.

Historically, refugees in the United States have made outstanding contributions to the economy and the social fabric of the nation. For example, it is estimated that 176,000 refugees are serving as health-care workers, and another 175,000 are working in the food supply chain. Refugees are essential workers in their communities. These and many other refugees and migrants in the United States distinguished themselves as frontline workers during the COVID-19 pandemic. Despite the COVID-19 pandemic, refugees, including myself, are covering critical appointments, serving as interpreters in high-risk areas such as hospitals and schools. We are moved by love and self-sacrifice. Additionally, numerous studies have revealed that resettled refugees contribute more to local host communities through taxes, public service, entrepreneurship, and volunteer service than they receive in initial benefits extended to them when they first arrive.

I am currently pastoring a congregation composed of Congolese who relocated to the United States of America through the United States Refugee Resettlement Program. They are finding that their living conditions are much improved, and they are making outstanding contributions to the national economic development through labor, employment creation, and payment of government taxes. Many refugees are testifying that they came to the United States as the result of God answering prayers because, besides helping themselves, they are also managing to send remittance to support their family members in their countries of origin. Therefore, they hope to achieve their dreams and build a better future for themselves, their children, and their grandchildren.

History on the origin of refugees and their protection institutions

The history of refugees and their protection is almost as old as human history. For instance, the Bible reveals various stories concerning some key people who were refugees. Among these were Jacob and his children, who left their country and lived in Egypt for four hundred years as refugees.

The God of Shadrach, Meshach, and Abednego was exalted when they were refugees or in captivity in Babylon. The Bible says, "Then Nebuchadnezzar said, "Praise be to the God of Shadrach, Meshach, and Abednego, who has sent his angel and rescued his servants! They trusted in him and defied the king's command and were willing to give up their lives rather than serve or worship any god except their own God. Therefore, I decree that the people of any nation or language who say anything against the God of Shadrach, Meshach and Abednego be cut into pieces and their houses be turned into piles of rubble, for no other god can save in this way" (Daniel 3:28–29).

At an early age, Jesus Christ of Nazareth was rushed to Egypt when an angel warned Joseph in a dream that King Herod planned to kill all the babies in Bethlehem (Matthew 2: 14–15). After the death and ascension of Jesus Christ, His disciples were persecuted. As a result, some were internally displaced, and others were forced to cross their national borders and live in foreign countries. While persecution was meant to harm them, God changed their situations for good because they spread the good news and planted churches everywhere and the kingdom of God was expanded.

Meanwhile, contemporary history of refugees and their protection can be traced back to the League of Nations, which existed from 1920 to 1946. The League of Nations, which was headquartered in Geneva, Switzerland, aimed to maintain global peace and security and promote international cooperation. Though the League of Nations achieved some remarkable success, it was unable to prevent the even deadlier World War II and was replaced by today's United Nations.

The United Nations was initiated in 1942 by Winston Churchill and Franklin D. Roosevelt in the Declaration by United Nations. This declaration was made to officially state the cooperation of the Allies (Great

Britain, the United States, and the Union of Soviet Socialist Republics) and other nations during World War II (UN Report 2011, 1).

> The United Nations was officially launched on October 24, 1945, in San Francisco, California. The United Nations High Commissioner for Refugees is a recognized international agency for refugee protection. The mandate of UNHCR is to protect the rights of refugees and to find solutions to their plight. To achieve this mission, it works in close collaboration with the hosting country and other humanitarian agencies to provide protection and emergency assistance such as water, food, shelter, medical service, education and other long-terms services for building livelihoods and a better future and hope for refugees across the world. Meanwhile, a former Director of Protection for UNHCR Geneva office traced the beginning of refugees and their protection to World War I (1914–1918), its preliminaries (the Balkan Wars, 1912–1913), and its aftermath in the Near East (the wars in the Caucasus, 1918–1921, and the Greco-Turkish War, 1919–1922). (Jaega 2001, 1)

During the above periods, an estimated "1 to 2 million war victims left Russian later Soviet territories for various countries in Europe or Asia Minor, Central and East Asia between 1918 and 1922 and also thereafter" (Jaega 2001, 1). Looking back to 1783 and prior to World War I, catastrophic events in the Ottoman Empire affected various ethno-religious communities including Muslim groups. In 1881, Russia saw the killing of Tsar Alexander II, which unleashed a wave of atrocious anti-Jewish sentiment in Russia. Poor economic performance and irresponsible press coverage had encouraged the notion of the Jew as the enemy, resulting in three years of rioting and prevalent attacks on Jewish homes. Approximately two decades later, latent injustice was revealed again when Jews were once again attacked, and thousands of innocent people were killed. The atrocious treatment of Jews prompted their massive exodus, and about two million of them fled to the United States, the United Kingdom, and other European countries.

UNHCR (2010) reveals that during the year 1914, Germany invaded Belgium, resulting in the massacre of thousands of civilians and the destruction of properties. Due to insecurity and fear of persecution, more than one million people were forced to flee their country and habitual residence and found asylum in other countries. Some of the largest carnage committed during World War I and World War II was directed at the Armenians. Millions of people were decimated by what was later recognized as the first genocide of the twentieth century. These miserable and atrocious events resulted in a humanitarian catastrophe, human vulnerability marking the early beginning of refugees. *The Guardian* (2011) estimated that, by the end of World War II, there were more than 40 million refugees in Europe alone. The scale of the disaster was such that international law and international organizations tasked to deal with refugees were urgently created and quickly evolved to become the foundation that is still relied upon in our present days.

One of the institutions created was named the International Refugee Organization (IRO). "IRO was created on 15 December 1946 by Resolution 62 (I) of the UN General Assembly; it initially worked as the Preparatory Commission for the IRO from 14 July 1947 to 20 August 1948 and then as full IRO from August 1948 until its termination on 28 February 1952" (Jaega 2001, 1).

Although most early movement and refugee events recorded were based in European countries, Africa was heavily hit by the slave trade. From that time to date, Africa has continued to experience widespread interstate and intrastate violent conflicts. Conflicts have plagued the Democratic Republic of Congo, Rwanda, Burundi, Uganda, Central Africa Republic, Eretria, Ethiopia, Somalia, South Sudan, Mali, and Mozambique, to name just a few. All these countries are still experiencing insecurity, causing millions of citizens to cross their national borders and live in exile as refugees in other countries. This is mainly because their home countries have been overtaken by violence, bad governance, poor leadership, and human rights violations, which contribute to underdevelopment, hunger, diseases, destruction of infrastructure, sexual exploitation, gender-based violence, and extreme poverty.

A 2020 UNHCR report estimates that there are over eight million people of concern to UNHCR. Most are people at risk from armed conflicts and political violence in their communities and countries of origin. Some of these war victim refugees are currently hosted in Southern Africa countries, including in Zimbabwe.

My view is that, if political leaders, especially in Africa and other countries affected by war would practice good leadership; democratic principles; and good economic governance based on transparency, accountability, equity, participation, pluralism, and the rule of law in an effective, efficient, and enduring manner, there would be a reduction in violent conflicts experienced across Africa. In practice, these principles can be interpreted in terms of "holding of free, fair, credible and frequent elections, representative legislatures that make laws and provides oversight, and an independent judiciary to interpret those laws" (UN 2013:1). These principles are also stipulated in the African Charter for Democracy, Elections and Governance. However, the missing gap is practice. When these principles are practiced by African leaders, they can enable governments to make good investment and use of abundant resources toward economic development, poverty alleviation, employment creation, and transformation of lives through the promotion of a high standard of living and human development. This situation can also reduce pressures on scarce services and resources, which at times generate conflicts between refugees and the local population in some refugee hosting countries in Africa.

Factors contributing to the increase of refugees

These factors include conflicts and wars between and within nations, which are more pronounced in Africa, the Middle East, and Asia. Most of these conflicts and wars are insurgents in nature, continuous and foreign-sponsored, showing no sign of being resolved. Castles (2003) states that northern economic interests play a role in perpetuating local wars while also contributing to underdevelopment in the south through their trade and intellectual property regimes. As a result, wars and civil strife have been there for years, making it difficult for many refugees to return to their countries of origin and habitual residence.

Durable solutions for refugees are viewed as threefold, namely voluntary repatriation, local integration, and resettlement of a refugee to the third country. There is a great need for the United State government, churches, and other religious groups; American business companies and their leaders; civil society organizations; the United Nations; world leaders; and nations to join hands and contribute to uprooting the root causes of wars and conflicts. They should promote peaceful conflict resolution through multitrack diplomacy for peacemaking, peacekeeping, and peace building. Ensuring the respect of human life and restoration of human dignity, good governance, justice, fair and mutually beneficial trade, and economic cooperation can ultimately lead to sustainable peace and development in countries affected by war and the world at large. In case of noncompliance by conflict parties, peace enforcement should be used as a last resort through UN Security Council chapter VII in cooperation with regional and national organizations responsible for mediation and peace building.

The plight of refugees in Africa

The Organization for African Unity (1969, 1) defines a refugee as "every person who, owing to external aggression, occupation, foreign domination, or events seriously disturbing public order in either part or the whole of his country of origin or nationality, is compelled to leave his place of habitual residence to seek refuge in another place outside his country of origin or nationality".

On the other hand, an asylum seeker is "someone who has made a claim that he/she is a refugee, and he/she is waiting for that claim to be accepted or rejected" (UNHCR 2007, 10).

Researchers and institutions involved in African conflicts mapping have identified various sources of conflicts affecting the African continent. These include but aren't limited to "underdevelopment, extreme poverty, human rights violations, bad governance, identity-based divisions and small arms proliferation" (Juma and Al 2006, vii). In addition, Heyns (2006) noted that the sources of conflicts in Africa are related to common experiences, which include colonial legacies, internal struggles, external interference, economic factors, poverty, security, and neo-patrimonialism. Jinadu explained that "prevailing conditions of scarcity, together with other impeding factors in the historical and current context—such as the impact of the colonial heritage and the workings of the international system—block the process of forming a de facto strong and inclusive state based on the classic ideals of the Weberian model. The sought-after separation of the state from society—the depersonalization of politics—thus becomes difficult, if not impossible. Centralist forms of rule, therefore, tend to facilitate regime behavior that fuels exclusivism, patronage, and state pilfering, reinforce hierarchical structures and breed inequality, marginalization, exclusion, and discrimination in various forms" (Jinadu 2007, 5).

Violent conflicts are a key impediment to the achievement of the United Nations Sustainable Development Goals in many African countries. The UN's Global Goals aim to end poverty, protect the planet, and ensure prosperity for everyone by 2030. The shocking effects of African conflicts include internal displacement; death of innocent persons, mainly civilians; sexual exploitation and gender-based violence; loss and destruction of property and infrastructure; poverty; and corruption. Conflicts contribute to high unemployment and interruption of economic development programs. In addition, the costs of peacemaking, peacekeeping and peace building in conflict-affected countries and managing refugees across borders, as well as ensuring human security can be viewed as contributing factors to challenges affecting Africa. This is making it difficult for many refugee-hosting countries, especially in Africa, to cope with the needs of refugees scattered in many countries on the African continent and beyond.

Bowd et al. (2010) has revealed that the countries of sub-Saharan Africa that have been embroiled in violent conflicts are characterized by abject poverty, inadequate service provision, political instability, retarded economic growth, and other challenges to overall development that deter the enhancement of human security. This situation perpetuates the plight of refugees, especially young people who, in most cases, constitute the most persons affected by war.

To establish peace and security in Africa, various intergovernmental and subregional agencies, such as the Southern Africa Development Community (SADC), Economic Community for West African States (ECOWAS), and the Panel of the Wise are working hand in hand with the African Union's Peace and Security Council (PSC) and the United Nations. In addition, the initiative by the New Partnership for Africa's Development (NEPAD) and the planned African Stand-by Force (ASF) is also a welcome development that can significantly contribute to addressing African crises and conflicts and, at the same time, finding African solutions to African problems. Due to the complexity of wars and international crises, the United States and the international community in developed countries need to play a significant role in capacity building for African leadership, government institutions, and civil society and help them to find durable solutions to refugee problems. To fulfill their international solidarity, many countries are hosting refugees.

Refugee camps in Africa

According to UNHCR (2013), except for Angola and South Africa, many countries in Southern and East Africa hosting a significant number of refugees uphold encampment policies that confine the freedom of movement of refugees and asylum seekers and hinder their efforts to become self-reliant. Most of these camps have been in existence for decades, and the second and sometimes third generations of refugees living in them find it difficult to envision a better future.

UNHCR's 2021 statistical report reveals that Uganda is one of the largest refugee-hosting nations in the world, with 1,450,317 refugees (as of February 2021). Kenya is hosting 508,033 persons of concern to the UNCHR (as of the end of January 2021). The majority of refugees and asylum seekers in Kenya originate from Somalia (54 percent). Other major nationalities are South Sudanese (24.6 percent), Congolese (9 percent), and Ethiopians (5.8 percent). Persons of concern from other nations, including Sudan, Rwanda, Eritrea, Burundi, Uganda, and others make up 6.8 percent of the total population. Almost half of the refugees in Kenya in refugee camps (44 percent) reside in Dadaab, 40 percent in Kakuma and 16 percent in urban areas (mainly Nairobi), alongside 18,500 stateless persons. While Kenya has been facing a lot of challenges in addressing social, economic, political, and security needs of its own citizens, refugee influx has added a burden and challenges to national security, as well as social and economic needs for both citizens and refugee community in Kenya.

Meanwhile, Botswana, Namibia, Tanzania, Zambia, and South Africa also host hundreds of thousands of refugees from different countries. Botswana and Namibia host refugees mostly from Zimbabwe, the Great Lakes countries, and other nations. South Africa is the biggest economic power in the African region, currently hosting a high number of refugees on the continent, most of them living in urban areas.

However, the low national economic performance experienced by many refugee-hosting countries in Africa, along with the low capacity to meet the needs and demands of their own citizens in terms of the provision of adequate employment opportunities and other social services required for basic human needs and human development has resulted in competition and conflicts in terms of seeking and securing jobs for sustainable livelihoods among nationals and vulnerable refugees. For instance, in South Africa, this situation resulted in xenophobic attacks and cruel killing of disadvantaged refugees, asylum seekers, and immigrants. In addition, thousands were displaced. During the xenophobic attacks, refugees, asylum seekers, and immigrants were burned to death, stubbed with machetes, and their belonging lotted and destroyed by angry South Africans. This situation should not be allowed to continue.

There is need for the South African government to ensure the protection of vulnerable refugees and other foreigners through the rule of law, retributive justice, and respect for human life. The cultural values of Ubuntu and solidarity that characterize Africans need to be instilled and reinforced among young generations. Also, it is important to teach the young people in South Africa the fact that, during the apartheid, South Africans were also refugees and asylum seekers in other African countries. In addition, many South Africans are currently living and working in other countries. Moreover, many African countries and people were directly involved and made significant contributions toward South Africa liberation from apartheid and colonialism. So we need each other.

We need to support one another in the spirit of brotherhood, bearing in mind that we are all the children of God. Jesus Christ said, "A new command I give you: Love one another. As I have loved you, so you must love one another. By this everyone will know that you are my disciples if you love one another" (John 13:34–35 NIV). Also, the Bible says, "Love the Lord your God with all your heart and with all your soul and with all your mind and with all your strength. The second is this: Love your neighbor as yourself. There is no commandment greater than these" (Luke 12:30–31 NIV). The love for God and for our neighbors must prevail.

Refugee rights convention

The 1951 Refugee Convention Articles 17 and 18 provide refugees the access and right to wage-earning employment and self-employment. In addition, Articles 20 to 24 of the 1951 Refugee Convention also provide for refugee access to rationing, housing, public education, public relief, labor legislation, and social security. Refugee-hosting countries have the responsibility to protect refugees, prevent refugee crimes, and fulfill the protection and provision of essential services and long-term solutions to enable vulnerable refugees, especially youths, to move away from being liabilities and toward being assets.

Access to formal education, vocational skills development courses, and decent employment via self-reliance initiatives can contribute to refugees' empowerment. In addition, the provision of such needs may enable young refugees to meaningfully contribute to the national development in their hosting countries and to participate, directly and indirectly, in peace building, leadership, governance, and reconstruction of their countries of origin in the future.

Background of Zimbabwe and refugee issues

Zimbabwe is a landlocked country of 390,580 square kilometers. Based on World meter's(2021) report, reveals that the current population of Zimbabwe is 14,986,707. Despite the change of government and leadership, the Zimbabwean economic crisis is deepening, especially the shortage of essential goods, as well as declining real wages amid soaring inflation, underlining the risk of wider political instability. Zimbabwe's political and economic challenges started soon after the fast-track land reform program of 2000. Since then, the country has not recovered economically. In January 2021, Zimbabwe's government extended lockdown due to coronavirus (COVID-19), exacerbating long-standing structural issues. As of January 6, 2021, Zimbabwe had 17,804 confirmed cases, including 11,966 recoveries and 431 deaths. Protests about the deepening economic crisis are increasing. The president, Emmerson Mnangagwa, and his government are trying their best, but the country's economy has remained weak, with worsening unemployment, food shortages, and poverty. As a result, many people are leaving the country.

Zimbabwe is a producer of and, at the same time, a destination for refugees. As a producer of refugees, "millions of Zimbabweans have left the country and are living in neighboring countries and overseas as refugees and asylum seekers" (UNHCR 2009). Research findings by Solidarity Peace Trust and PASSOP (2012, 5) estimate that up to 1.4 million South African refugees and asylum seekers are Zimbabweans. This number might have since doubled considering the deepening crisis.

On the other hand, Zimbabwe has extended its hospitality and international solidarity and is currently hosting war victim refugees and asylum seekers, as well as economic refugees in transit to South Africa, where they seek greener pastures. Zimbabweans are among the well-educated people in the Southern African region. They are patriotic, hospitable, hardworking, and peace-loving. Agriculture is the backbone of the Zimbabwean economy. Also, the country is vested with majestic tourism attraction sites such as Victoria Falls, which is one of the seven natural wonders of the world. Zimbabwe has abundant natural resources that can be used to transform its economy if supported politically and internationally.

My advice to my fellow Zimbabweans is that. despite economic and political challenges, every Zimbabwean must cherish peace and avoid violence. "Weeping may stay for the night but rejoicing comes in the morning" (Psalm 30:5 NIV). Your morning is coming; just keep trusting God in prayer and working harder and smarter. One day, Zimbabwe will rise and shine again.

Given the above discussions, one can view the refugee issue as a political, leadership, and governance problem. It is political because its solution requires political will and commitment. It is a leadership and governance problem because its solution requires democratic government institutions, policies, and effective political leadership. Like many other African countries, Zimbabwe need a fundamental change of mindset in order to rebuild and reform the nation's institutional capacity and capabilities.

Therefore, I am more concerned with refugee youth and their access to educational opportunities and sustainable livelihoods that can enable them to gain knowledge, experience, and income and achieve their potentials. What this means is that, if opportunities are created, refugees can be groomed and become leaders and industrialists.

States' responsibility to protect refugees

According to UNHCR (2013), the international human rights law and international refugee law provides that states have the primary obligation for refugee protection. As a result, in most countries UNHCR partners with governments and their respective ministries to ensure the protection and provision of essential services to refugees. Zimbabwe is a signatory to the 1951 United Nations Convention Relating to the Status of Refugees and its 1967 Protocol and to the 1969 Organization for Africa Unity (OAU now AU) Convention governing the specific aspects of refugee problems in Africa, which was ratified and domesticated through the Refugee Act, chapter 4:03 on October 28, 1983.

However, one needs to acknowledge that Zimbabwe has experienced over a decade of political and economic challenges. Currently, it is estimated that "over 80% of Zimbabwean work force is out of formal employment" (Southern Eye, April 26, 2020, 1). What this means is that the Zimbabwe government has its own challenges in meeting the needs and demands of its citizens.

Nevertheless, when refugees run away from their country of origin, they dream of finding peace, protection, and a better life in their country of asylum. Such a dream can only be achieved when opportunities for personal development, actualization, and transcendence are created through enabling environments, policies, and practices. This research will establish whether such opportunities and favorable policies are provided to youth refugees living in Tongogara Refugee Camp.

Conclusion

This chapter has given the background to the study, which focused on the plight of refugees in the world, with a particular focus on Africa. The history of refugees, contributing factors and refugee protection institutions, and refugee laws and conventions were also given. It provided an explanation of the challenges experienced by refugees in refugee camps. The chapter has also given an explanation of why Zimbabwe is considered both a producer of and a destination for refugees. It provided information on states' responsibility to protect refugees and the outstanding role played by the US government in welcoming refugees through refugee resettlement programs.

The chapter also detailed the contributions being made by refugees to the US economy. And a table showing ceilings for refugee arrivals in the United States from 2010 through 2021 was given. The next chapter will focus on human needs theory and how it relates to the refugee situation.

CHAPTER 4

HUMAN NEEDS THEORY

Introduction

This chapter looks at a range of available literature on refugees in general and refugee youth access to educational opportunities and sustainable livelihoods. It attempts to give an analysis of what has been written by other scholars and writers about refugees and their access to education and livelihoods. The study is informed by the human needs theory (HNT), psychologist Abraham Maslow (1908–1970), and conflict scholar John Burton (1915–2010). Emphasis will be placed on John Burton.

Both Maslow and Burton have emphasized that "human needs are not limited to food, water and clothing; they include physical and non-physical aspects for human development and growth" (Maslow 1970, Burton 1990). There are different types of needs, which can be categorized as comparative needs, felt needs, and normative needs. Felt needs are needs that one cannot do without their fulfillment, and these are nonnegotiable needs. Typical examples may be the need for food, medical care, clothing, and shelter. The absence of felt needs can result in physical death or starvation of the human being. In terms of community development, felt needs are real needs that require attention to enable a human being to stay alive. The absence of felt needs may lead to absolute poverty, vulnerability, powerlessness, and isolation, and it is an abuse of essential human rights. On the other hand, Australia Research Alliance for Child and Youth argues, "Comparative needs are needs relative to other groups, whereas, felt needs, are what an individual wants, and normative need are what others define as the needs of an individual or group" (Australia Research Alliance for Child and Youth 2007, 9).

The theory of human needs states that every human being needs certain essentials to live and attain well-being. These are called human needs or basic human needs. Maslow's basic needs theory has a long-standing tradition in motivation research and practice. As the term suggests, "The theory focuses on what people require to live fulfilling lives" (Stoner and Al 2006, 447).

Burton (1990) argued that conflicts and violent conflicts are principally caused by unmet human needs. He further explained that violence happens when certain individuals or groups do not see any other way to meet their needs or when they need understanding, respect, and consideration for their needs. Access to education and sustainable livelihoods can be viewed as essential human needs that every human being must be entitled to and are cornerstones for achieving human development and self-reliance. Burton and Maslow presented human needs, ranking them as summarized in table 1.

Table 2: Human needs ranking as presented by Maslow and Burton

Maslow	Burton
Food, water, shelter	Distributive justice
Safety and security	Safety, security
Belonging or love	Belonging or love
Self-esteem	Self-esteem
Self-actualization	Persona fulfilment
	Cultural security, freedom, participation

Source: Danielsen (2005)

To better discuss each of the above needs presented by Maslow and Burton, the researcher looked at each author separately and will later link their views and models to the current study.

Maslow's hierarchy of needs

Stoner and Al (2006, 448) described Maslow's hierarchy of needs—a five-stage model—as follows: *"Physiological needs are requirements for human survival. They include breathing, food, water, shelter, sex, clothing, and sleep.*

Second needs in Maslow's needs theory ranking include safety and/or security needs. These needs can be viewed as meeting future physiological needs and include protection, personal and financial security, order, law, stability, and freedom of movement and choice. These two are the most fundamental and vital human needs. They are followed by social needs for love and belonging and self-esteem needs to feel worthy, respected, and have status. The final and highest-level needs are self-actualization needs or self-fulfillment and achievement" These ambitious and critical needs can come from peace, knowledge, and self-fulfillment and realization of personal potential, personal growth, and peak experiences.

Relevance of Maslow's hierarchy of needs theory to the study

Each stage of the five levels of Maslow's hierarchy of needs given in table. 1 applies to the context of this study. This is considering that, in most cases, when a war victim refugee leaves his or her country of origin, she or he leaves without anything and becomes a vulnerable person. Additionally, some of the needs mentioned by Maslow, such as physiological and safety needs, are essential for human survival and, therefore, not negotiable. They apply equally to every human being, despite their social, political, and economic status.

Biological and physiological needs for refugees

From time to time, war victim refugees travel long distances in dangerous conditions and, therefore, leave all their valuable things and property behind. When they arrive in a country of asylum, their first and fundamental needs are biological, physiological, and safety needs. Biological and physiological needs, which are basic life needs for refugees include the need for shelter, food, water, medical care, and sleep. UNHCR, together with other humanitarian agencies, work hand in hand with the states that host refugees and their related ministries and departments in ensuring that refugees get access to necessities to meet their human needs on arrival.

Safety needs

Refugee-hosting states are expected to play the leading role in providing safety needs, which include protection, security, order, law, stability, and freedom.

Impact of refugee encampment policy on security and freedom of movement

In most sub-Saharan African countries except South Africa, most refugees are living in refugee camps. In Zimbabwe, refugees are confined to Tongogara Refugee Camp. This is in line with the provision of section 12 of the Refugee Act, encampment policy. Where refugees should reside in Zimbabwe is determined by the responsible minister of labor and social welfare. In this case, Tongogara Refugee Camp is the only sanctuary designated to house refugees in Zimbabwe.

Kenya, Zambia, and Tanzania are also among African countries that restrict hundreds of thousands of refugees in refugee camps.

According to the 2021 UNHCR report, the United Republic of Tanzania hosts 287,903 refugees. The Western province of Kigoma hosts 259,297 refugees; Katavi, 21,448; Tabora, 6,742; Dar es Salaam, 266; and Tanga, 150 (as of January 30, 2021). Most refugees (over 90 percent) are living in refugee camps. Many of them are from Burundi and the DRC. The same UNCHR report reveals that chronic underfunding has resulted in serious gaps in the provision of humanitarian assistance to refugees hosted in Tanzania.

Refugee movement and access to employment are restricted. They rely on humanitarian aid, which increases their dependence, poverty, vulnerability, isolation, and powerlessness. Many refugees are reduced to one meal a day and sometimes two meals in four days, because monthly food ration provided by the UNHCR is limited. Access to clean water and quality education is also a challenge. Refugees in the camps have no access to electricity. Most refugees have been living in miserable, hopeless, and humbling conditions in camps for five to more than twenty years.

I am currently pastoring a congregation composed of refugees, 80 percent of whom lived in Nyarugusu Refugee Camp in Tanzania before relocating to the United States. They always share their stories on their long-term encampment and difficult living conditions experienced in Nyarugusu Refugee Camp. Some of the testimonies are covered in chapter nine of this book.

However, many scholars in refugee and international human rights law studies are worried about the long-term encampment of the vulnerable refugees. "While these individuals might be given the right to life through the principle of *non-refoulement*, the cornerstone of international refugee law, this right has come at the expense of other fundamental human rights that are directly jeopardized by policies of long-term encampment" (Refugee Law Initiative 2012, 1).

Explaining the painful experience of staying for a long time in a refugee camp, a Sudanese female refugee who lived in Kakuma Refugee Camp in Kenya said, "Kakuma is desert county with extremely hot weather. We had little food and water, and we were always hungry. It is a violent place where many people are raped and murdered. We lived in Kakuma camp for 8 years; we looked for resettlement and prayed to God for help every day" (Sanctuary Australia Foundation 2013, 2). What this means is that, while refugees leave their home countries to seek asylum in other countries and hope for protection and better living conditions, life in refugee camps can be crueler, more insecure, and more degrading than the situations they fled.

When refugees are restricted to a camp, they have no freedom of movement outside their restricted areas. However, Article 12 of the International Covenant for Civil and Political Rights, the Universal Declaration of Human Rights, the 1951 Geneva Convention, and its 1967 Protocol provide for freedom of movement. Restricting refugee movement undermines international law and refugee law. Meanwhile, scholars in international law and refugee studies believe that freedom of movement is necessary to fulfill a host of fundamental civil, political, social, and economic human rights. This right is being denied in long-term camps where the host state either in law and/or in practice arbitrarily denies such freedom by, for example, "using the system of exit passes and leaving some refugees for decades in a de facto state of aid dependency and physical confinement" UNHCR 2015)

The practice of gate pass is also evident in Nyarugusu Refugee Camp based in the western province of Kigoma, United Republic of Tanzania, and in Tongogara Refugee Camp, whereby refugees are asked to apply for one if they want to travel outside the camp. The authority in the camp has the right to accept or reject the application. If a refugee is caught by a police officer or an immigration officer outside the camp without the gate pass, he or she is arrested and sometimes deported, even if the person has valid documentations. Restriction of movement undermines security and safety

Dr. Joseph Boomenyo

needs and the right to freedom of movement guaranteed by the 1951 United Nations Refugee Convention.

Belongingness needs

The sense of belonging, togetherness, or attachment is incredibly significant to war victim refugees. It takes courage to be a refugee, and one must overcome many obstacles. When one has been forced to leave his or her home country and finds himself or herself in a foreign country as a refugee, he or she becomes vulnerable, having lost his or her social networks and assets. Most refugee camps are characterized by a multicultural environment, with many unaccompanied children and separated families. Refugee-hosting countries and the UNHCR have the primary mandate to accept refugees and make them feel at home away from home through settlement and integration into society. In most cases, new arrival refugees are traumatized because of war and concern for life. This situation makes refugees vulnerable, as such they need much care and love, which gives them a sense of belonging.

Maslow views belongingness needs in terms of being loved and loving others; belonging to a family; enjoying affection; developing good relationships with others in different social situations, including but not limited to work, school, sport clubs, associations, and churches. Some refugee hosting countries are open and hospitable in terms of accepting and loving refugees. However, in other countries, refugees are viewed as enemies and not welcomed by average local people. The hatred for refugees in South Africa was expressed in 2008, 2010, and 2018, when unemployed South African youth carried out xenophobic attack against refugees and foreigners; both documented and undocumented were affected. In analyzing the underlying causes of the xenophobic attacks that exploded in South Africa, Everett attributed it to "a combination of deep structural social, economic and spatial inequalities, an ongoing reliance on cheap labor, housing shortages, township retail competition, racism, a history of the use of violence to advance sectional interests, and a traumatically scarred national psyche combined in early 2008 with a desperately low national mood as the economy seemed to be in free fall and the ruling party was in the midst of factional splitting, to create ripe conditions for the xenophobic outburst" (Everett 2010, 2).

Article 14 (1) of the Universal Declaration of Human Rights, however, clarifies that, "Everyone has the rights to seek and to enjoy in other countries asylum from persecution. This means that refugees should be entitled to enjoy protection from persecution in their countries of asylum. They should also enjoy services that would enable them to effectively integrate in the society"(United Nations 1948, 1) Therefore, 'Refugees to Australia, for example, who come through its official resettlement program, receive some of the best government-funded settlement services in the world. These services cater to their material, medical and, to some extent, their social needs" (University of Western Australia 2013, 2). This type of assistance and care contributes to one feeling a sense of belongingness and love. Love is the greatest commandment found in the Bible. The Bible says, "Anyone who hates a brother or sister is a murderer, and you know that no murderer has eternal life residing in him. This is how we know what love is: Jesus Christ laid down his life for us. And we ought to lay down our lives for our brothers and sisters. If anyone has material possessions and sees a brother or sister in need but has no pity on them, how can the love of God be in that person?" (1 John 3:15–17). The principle of loving our brothers, sisters, and strangers is critical for harmonious living in families, communities, and society, and it is pleasing to God. If we hate our own brothers and sisters, we are murderers.

Women's Self-Promotion Movement (WSPM), which is a women empowerment organization that works with refugees in Zimbabwe and Western Tanzania, revealed that a dominating patriarchal system in the management of some refugee camps contributes to gender blindness and the perpetuation of traditional practices that continue to entrench unequal opportunities between men and women in access to, ownership and control of economic, social, and physical resources. These practices result in women being dependent on men for survival. Unfortunately, this dependability encourages men to view women as economic and social instruments, thus making women powerless in the face of forced marriages, domestic violence, coercion, sexualized gender abuse, hunger, promiscuous partners, and general women's rights abuses in Tongogara and in Nyarugusu Refugee Camps. (WSPM Report 2012, 7)

Many governments, especially in Africa, keep refugees in camps, fearing the economic and security burden of keeping them in towns and cities. In addition, refugee-hosting countries in Africa have been experiencing economic challenges to address the fundamental needs of their own citizens. This is making it difficult for many countries to provide an enabling environment, resources, and facilities for refugees to achieve a sense of belonging, consideration, and recognition. My research will establish whether youth refugees in Tongogara Refugee Camp have access to educational and sustainable livelihoods opportunities and how these contribute to a sense of belongingness and acceptance.

Esteem needs

Maslow viewed esteem needs in terms of achievement, status, responsibility, and reputation. All human beings, including refugees, have big dreams and desire to achieve great things in their personal, family, and community lives. These can only be achieved under favorable policies and economic environment and practices.

According to the Australian government (2010), after successful integration, refugees can make cultural, social, and economic contributions in their hosting country. Humanitarian entrants are often entrepreneurial as they establish themselves in a new environment. In 2000, five of Australia's eight billionaires were people whose forefathers had originally come to the country as refugees. This reality—the very real possibility of ultimate success of those who migrate in search of refuge—is also revealed in biblical records on refugees (for example, take the cases of Joseph in Egypt, Daniel in Babylon, and Nehemiah in the Persian royal court).

Meanwhile, Milner (2011), in "New Issues in Refugee Research," reveals that refugees can make positive contributions to peace building in their country of origin if they benefit from skills training and self-reliance while in exile. This is to say, if opportunities are created, not only can refugees and/or foreigners in exile positively contribute to promoting durable development in their hosting countries. They can also participate in the national reconstruction of their countries of origin in the future when they go back and even through remittance to their families back home and direct participation in governance, leadership consultancy, business creation, investment, and missions while still away. The researcher will establish whether this policy is applicable to refugees in Tongogara Camp and any other refugee camp around the world.

Due to dynamics in research, development, and scholarly criticism, other scholars and business consulting companies such as Business Balls (www.businessballs.com), adapted eight levels of hierarchy of needs diagram based on Maslow's. The eight-level diagram lists needs ranging from physiological needs, safety needs, and love and belongingness needs to esteem needs, cognitive needs, aesthetic needs, and self-actualization needs and, finally, transcendence needs, which means seeking to help others achieve self-actualization.

Burton's human needs theory and its relevance to the study

Burton (1990) views satisfying universal human needs as key to prevent or resolve social and political conflicts. He looks at how universal human needs are often neglected, leading groups to use violence to claim their rights and satisfy their needs. In his view, the needs most critical to an understanding of destructive social conflicts are those for identity, recognition, security, and personal development. Burton looked at distributive justice, safety, and security, belonging and love, self-esteem, personal fulfillment, cultural security, freedom, and participation. Most of these are already explained in Maslow's hierarchy of needs. This section will only focus on the aspects that Burton added to the human needs theory.

Cultural security

Cultural security is related to identity—the need for recognition of one's language, traditions, religion, cultural values, ideas, and concepts. Refugees in asylum countries need to be culturally recognized by practicing their tradition, religion, ideas, and concepts.

Freedom

Burton views freedom as the condition of having no physical, political, or civil restraints and having the capacity to exercise choice in all aspects of one's life. This need can only be achieved if refugees are granted permanent residence or naturalization as practiced in South Africa and most Western countries.

Distributive justice

Distributive justice is the need for the fair allocation of resources among all members. It focuses on adopting positive measures to ensure that all policies, whether economic, social, cultural, or legal, benefit all members equally. Refugees in countries of asylum should also be viewed as equal members of the society with needs to be met and, therefore, the need for distributive justice.

Participation

Burton views participation as the need to be able to actively partake in and influence civil society. Refugee law provides for the need for refugees to participate in public life, especially when they have been granted permanent residence and citizenship and can influence civil society and national economy. Typical examples are France, where people who were received as refugees had made significant contribution through exhibiting their talents in sport, and in Australia, where five out of eight billionaires in 2000 were people, whose ancestors had come to Australia as refugees.

Similarities and differences between Maslow and Burton

The two theow, and Burton, seemed to share the same ideas in their theoretical approach, but Burton seemed to have borrowed some ideas from Maslow. However, even if there are some similarities in the theories, the emphasis is different. Burton added some aspects in building his theory, which are cultural security, distributive justice, freedom, and participation.

Conclusion

This chapter discussed the human needs theory and its importance to this study that seeks to establish the range of educational and sustainable livelihoods available to youth refugees in Tongogara Refugee Camp. The major lesson learned is that every human being has needs. Some needs are not negotiable, and others are negotiable. Human needs range from basic life needs, namely physiological and biological needs, to the highest needs for recognition, achievement, self-actualization, and transcendence. Access to educational and sustainable livelihood opportunities can significantly contribute to the empowerment of young refugees and, ultimately, enable them to become valuable resources to the community and the nations to which they belong, both their home nations and their host nations.

CHAPTER 5

LIVING CONDITIONS OF REFUGEES IN TONGOGARA REFUGEE CAMP IN ZIMBABWE

History and Location of Tongogara Refugee Camp

Tongogara Refugee Camp was established in 1982, in line with the provisions of Section 12 of Refugee Act (chapter 4:03), Zimbabwe Government Encampment Policy. The camp was named after the national liberation fighter, Josiah Magama Tongogara, who was born in 1933 and died on December 26, 1979. Basically, the camp was established for a rehabilitation of ex-combatants of 1980. From 1986 to 1992, the camp provided accommodation to Mozambican refugees. After the end of the war in Mozambique, the camp was reopened in 1996 and catered to street children and single mothers. In 1998, the Zimbabwean government designated Tongogara Refugee Camp as the residence for all refugees and asylum seekers. The camp has the capacity to accommodate 3,000 people but there were 14,300 refugees and asylum seekers living in the camp (as of January 2021).

The camp is provided with borehole water and a medical clinic, which provides basic medical services. In case of health complications, ill refugees are transferred to Chipinge Hospital. The UNHCR built a few bricks and wooden houses for refugee accommodation. However, due to the influx of new arrivals, the camp became overcrowded, and accommodation becomes a crisis. As a result, most refugees are building their own huts and houses using mud. Tents are also provided for temporary shelter.

The weakness of keeping people in the camp is that doing so creates a dependence syndrome in which people come to depend on humanitarian aid in terms of food handouts and can also perpetuate vulnerability and laziness. Confinement can also result in starvation, especially when the humanitarian aid is reduced or cut off. However, livelihood sustainability can only be achieved through initiatives that help people to help themselves. In other words, when you give someone a fish, he or she will eat for a day, but if you teach that person to fish, he or she will eat forever.

Number of asylum seekers and refugees in Tongogara Refugee Camp

According to the UNHCR (2021) statistics, 14,300 people were living in Tongogara Refugee Camp (as of December 31, 2020). Most of them were refugees and asylum seekers from Burundi, Rwanda, Congo-Brazzaville, the Democratic Republic of Congo (DRC), Ethiopia, Mali, Syria and Somalia, South-Sudan, South Africa, Côte D'ivoire, Uganda, Tanzania, Ghana, Zambia, and Eritrea. The above statistics includes 111 Zimbabweans married to refugees.

It is important to mention that many refugee camps in the world are usually characterized by large, fenced areas lined with blue and while UNHCR emergency housing tents. But Tongogara is now a permanent camp. Therefore, most houses are made of mud and brick. More than half of the refugees there have lived in the camp for a long time—from five to more than twenty years. The camp is crowded, and living conditions are extremely hard.

Most refugees and asylum seekers were from the DRC

It was established that the influx of refugees from the DRC into Zimbabwe can be explained by a series of negative events, which has been manifested through horrible endless wars, loss of human life and property, rampant violation of human rights, and poverty and lawlessness that has affected the DRC for decades.

In June 1960, DRC became independent, with Patrice Emery Lumumba, a visionary leader, as prime minister and Joseph Kasa-Vubu as the first president. On January 17, 1961, six months after independence, Lumumba was killed in a military coup, possibly near Elizabethville, State of Katanga now Lubumbashi, which is the second largest city of the Democratic Republic of the Congo. Shortly after the assassination of Lumumba, the country experienced a series of rebellions and secessionist movements, sometimes with the direct encouragement of external actors. Shortly after the second parliamentary general elections, Colonel Mobutu Sese Seko successfully organized a coup and assumed power. Mobutu Sese Seko became president in 1965 and changed the name of the country from Congo to Zaire. He remained in power for thirty-two years.

In 1994, genocide in neighboring Rwanda claimed more than eight hundred thousand lives. A massive influx of hundreds of thousands of Rwandan refugees into eastern Zaire (now the Democratic Republic of the Congo), namely in South Kivu and North Kivu provinces, marked the beginning of instability in the DRC.

In 1996 and 1997, Rwanda, Uganda, and their sponsored rebel groups invaded Zaire, sparking the First Congo War. The autocratic regime of Mobutu Sese Seko was overthrown by an alliance, supposedly under the leadership of Laurent-Désiré Kabila and strongly backed by Rwanda, Uganda, and several other governments.

In January 2001, Kabila was assassinated and replaced by his son, Joseph Kabila, as president of the DRC. Joseph Kabila led the country for nineteen years and was succeeded by Félix Tshisekedi in the first peaceful transition of power in the history of the Democratic Republic of the Congo.

From 1997 to date, the war in DRC has resulted in the death of over 12 million civilians, mostly women and children. A United Nations Report (2011) revealed that 1,152 women are raped every day—a rate equal to forty-eight per hour. But a coalition of women's organizations in North Kivu and South Kivu provinces revealed that, every minute, five women and girls are either raped, killed, or mutilated. Many cases are unreported because of fear and death threats by perpetrators.

Some of the most acute violence and genocide in the country in recent years were caused by Banyamulenge and their allies, which took place in Makobala and several other places in Fizi district, South Kivu province in 1998 and still on up to date. For example, on Monday August 24, 1998, more than 800 people, mostly belonging to the Babembe community, were killed in Makobala village. Others were burned to death in places such as Kazimia, Fizi-Itombwe; Wimbi 3 or Akyumba in Tanganyika province. Fighting between various rebel groups such as Ngumino led by Makanika-Twigwaneho and their foreign allies; Mai mai militias and the Congolese army continue to disturb peace and security efforts in Epupu, Mienge, Minembwe and many other villages and towns. Many innocent people, especially women and children are being massacred, mutilated, raped, kidnapped, and burned to death. Properties, such as homes and livestock are also destroyed in a war devastated region of the high plateaus of Fizi-Itombwe-Uvira in south-Kivu province of the DRC).

Monusco (2020) report reveals the list of other active and illegal foreign armed groups operating on the soil of the DR Congo, which are *"the Democratic Forces for the Liberation of Rwanda (FDLR), the Allied Democratic Forces (ADF) is a Ugandan rebel group based along the Rwenzori Mountains of eastern DR Congo. The Lord's Resistance Army (LRA) is a Ugandan rebel group currently based along the northern border areas of Congo as well as in the eastern Central African Republic. The National Liberation Forces (FNL) is a Burundian rebel group originally formed in 1985 as the military wing of a Hutu-led rebel group called the PALIPEHUTU"*. All those rebel groups are currently disturbing peace and security in South Kivu province and other provinces in the DRC. There is need for the Congolese government to ensure the rule of law, safety, and security of all the people living in the DRC. Citizens and residents must learn to live at peace with each other and respect human life. I strongly believe that every citizen and resident of the DRC can prosper socially, and economically in the DRC without war. I am currently living in Fort Worth, Texas, USA. One of the lessons I am learning here is that people of Texas are prospering because of peace, security, strong government institutions and policies, the rule of law and the culture of hard working and commitment by individual citizens and residents. While our people are busy killing each other in the DRC, Americans are busy building soft and hard infrastructures. In this country, jobs and other resources are made available to everyone everywhere. Let's learn from the Americans. Let's have the abundance mindset and ensure that all Congolese benefit from their national resources without violence.

Other violence and genocide took place in Yumbi, western Congo, in mid-December 2018, when at least 535 people were killed. Most of the victims were ethnic Banunu, killed by ethnic Batende. In eastern Congo, several armed groups, and in some cases government security forces, attacked civilians, killing and wounding many. The humanitarian situation remained alarming, with 4.5 million people internally displaced, and more than 890,000 people from Congo were registered as refugees and asylum seekers. These are some of the factors that have contributed to the influx of refugees from the DRC into Zimbabwe and other countries throughout the world, including the United States of America.

United Nations Peacekeeping Presence in the DRC

According to the United Nations (1999), report, the United Nations Security Council deployed one of the biggest peacekeeping forces in the Democratic Republic of Congo. The UN peacekeeping force in the DRC was established by the United Nations Security Council in resolutions 1279 (1999) and 1291 (2000). The mission was known as the United Nations Mission in the Democratic Republic of Congo or MONUC, an acronym of its French name Mission de l'Organisation des Nations Unies en République Démocratique du Congo. Traditionally, the UN peacekeepers mandate is to contribute to the stabilization of some of the world's most volatile conflict zones, protecting civilians from violence; monitoring the implementation of peace agreements; disarming, demobilizing, and reintegrating former combatants into society. They facilitate the delivery of humanitarian assistance, training national police forces; and supporting free and fair elections, and the creating stable governing institutions.

The first UN presence in the Democratic Republic of the Congo, before the passing of Resolution 1291, was a force of military observers to observe and report on the compliance on factions with the peace accords, a deployment authorized by the earlier Resolution 1258 (1999). UN Security Council in resolutions 1279 (1999) and 1291 (2000) of the United Nations Security Council was meant to monitor the peace process of the Second Congo War, with a particular focus on Ituri and Kivu. The mandate of peacekeeping military, police, and civilian personnel deployed under MONUC continued until 2010, mainly focused on preventive diplomacy, peacemaking, and peacekeeping. MONUC was later replaced by the United Nations Organization Stabilization Mission in the Democratic Republic of the Congo or MONUSCO an acronym based on its French name (French: Mission de l'Organisation des Nations Unies pour la stabilisation en République démocratique du Congo). UN Security Council Resolution 2348 (2017) provided the authority for the current MONUSCO mandate, which include but not limited to contributing to the D.R Congo peacebuilding. Peacebuilding is about identifying and dealing with the root causes of conflicts and building the capacity of societies to manage their differences and conflicts without resorting to violence. It is about promoting positive peace. The aim is to prevent the outbreak, escalation, continuation, and recurrence of violence, so can take place before, during and after conflicts. It is a long-term and collaborative process, as it involves changes in attitudes, behaviors, and norms. It also involves national reconstruction by investing into social and economic reconstruction projects for national development. The following nations (in alphabetical order) contributed with military personnel: Bangladesh, Belgium, Benin, Bolivia, Bosnia and Herzegovina, Brazil, Burkina Faso, Cameroon, Canada, China, Côte d'Ivoire, Czech Republic, Egypt, France, Ghana, Guatemala, India, Indonesia, Ireland, Jordan, Kenya, Malawi, Malaysia, Mali, Mongolia, Morocco, Nepal, the Netherlands, Niger, Nigeria, Pakistan, Paraguay, Peru, Poland, Romania,

Russia, Senegal, Serbia, South Africa, Sri Lanka, Sweden, Switzerland, Tanzania, Tunisia, Ukraine, the United Kingdom, the United States, Uruguay, Yemen and Zambia. Meanwhile, the following nations contributed with police personnel: Bangladesh, Benin, Brazil, Burkina Faso, Cameroon, Chad, Egypt, France, Ghana, Guinea, Jordan, Madagascar, Mali, Niger, Nigeria, Romania, Russia, Senegal, Sweden, Switzerland, Togo, Tunisia, Turkey, Ukraine, and Yemen. From 1999, about nine billion United States dollars had been spent to fund the UN peacekeeping effort in the DRC by October 2017.

As of November 2021, the money spent to fund the UN peacekeeping effort in the DRC will possibly exceed $10 billion. Such expenses justify why and how peace keeping is one of the most expensive operations. "The total strength of UN peacekeeping troops in the DRC is approximately 18,300" (UN, 2019). This is probably the biggest and longest-serving UN peacekeeping mission deployed in one country since World War II.

Despite the presence of MONUSCO, the country's leadership has not managed to maintain peace and human security. Therefore, from 1994 to date, over 12 million civilians have died due to war in the DRC. In addition, instability continues to rise. As a result, many Congolese believe that MONUSCO has failed, and its mission in the DRC is now overdue. There have been various demonstrations by angry Congolese demanding the departure of MONUSCO. Such groups believe that MONUSCO is now part and parcel of the causes of the security problems and instability being experienced in the DRC in our present day.

Currently, most Congolese rely on the informal sector for a chance to earn a living. In addition, there is inadequate access to basic services, like energy, water and sanitation, education, health care, and agriculture. Over 60 percent of the population in the country lives below the poverty line, and many earn two dollars a day and less. Therefore, most Congolese believe that some of the funds channeled to the UN peacekeeping personnel in the DRC should have been used to support the above-named social and economic development projects. Also, other Congolese believe that part of the funds invested in the UN peacekeeping personnel should have been channeled to the training and capacity building of local security forces, namely military, police, and civilian, and more could have been used to build and maintain national roads and other important projects for national development. Others strongly believe that MONUSCO's presence is justified because the DRC security sector is not yet stable enough to run by itself. In my opinion, the deployment of the peacekeeping mission in the DRC was justified and can be viewed as an important intervention. The only challenge is that they have stayed longer than what was expected by the Congolese. What makes the matter worse is that despite their presence, the country has remained unstable.

The DRC as an economic power for Africa yet deeply rooted in poverty

The Democratic Republic of the Congo is the second largest African country, located in the subregion of Central Africa, with an estimated 87 million people. It shares borders with nine different countries, namely Tanzania, Zambia, Angola, Congo-Brazzaville, Central Africa Republic, South Sudan, Uganda, Rwanda, and Burundi. Although, the DRC is blessed with abundant natural resources, much of its population is still suffering due to instability, poverty, and unemployment.

Research by Suffolk University (2012) revealed that the DRC contains about $24 trillion worth of valuable minerals, such as coltan, gold, diamonds, tin, and uranium. This equals the combined gross domestic product of Europe and United States. But the DRC has fallen into what is described as a "resource curse" due to endless war, corruption, and lack of respect of human rights and impunity. An estimated $6 million in resources leaves the Congo every day through corrupt means. This situation should not be allowed to continue.

Currently, over 60 percent of Congolese are living in poverty and are unemployed. There is need for a change of mindset and action toward reviving national development through responsible governance, government, and leadership. Currently, many Congolese are hoping that the new government will create enabling policies and a favorable environment that will promote a new and strong partnership for social and economic development that will positively impact the living conditions and status of most of its population.

There is a need to invest, first and foremost, in peace and security. This will require the DRC government to capitalize on the training and capacity building of security officers. There is no development without sustainable peace, and peace cannot be achieved without development. After the training of officers, the government should have faith in them and ensure that the security officers receive reasonable, ordinary, acceptable, and competitive salaries and packages that will motivate them to effectively discharge their duties and be able to take care of their immediate family needs through their monthly salary. I am emphasizing this because currently the DRC security personnel, teachers, and health workers are among the most neglected and miserable workers, treated like beggars due to low and irregular remunerations. This unacceptable situation must be addressed by the current DRC government.

Additionally, there is a need for the restoration of an independent judicial system that will promote the rule of law, encourage respect of human rights and human life, and combat impunity. Credible, regular, and transparent elections must be held, and they must be administered by trusted independent election commissions and systems at local and national levels.

There is a need to invest in agriculture mechanization, rural industrialization, and electrification to improve food and nutritional security. Industries—including but not limited to mining, trade, and banking; road, air, maritime, and railway infrastructures and means of transportation; environmental protection and management; and science, technology, entrepreneurship, and other sectors—must be revived, which will create jobs.

There is need to invest in soft infrastructure to promote prosperity among Congolese and help the country to take off and achieve the stage of mass production. Soft infrastructure refers to all the services required to maintain the economic, health, and cultural and social standards of a population, as opposed to the hard infrastructure. Soft infrastructure includes institutions such as the education system, namely well-resourced colleges, and universities; the financial system; the health care system; the system of government; and law enforcement and emergency services. Hard infrastructure is tangible or built infrastructure such as roads, buildings, airports and bridges.

The DRC needs industrialization, strong regional integration, and competitiveness. These can contribute to turning our country from an exporter of minerals and primary products to a key regional and global player and exporter of processed goods. Most importantly, there is a need for a change of mindset among all Congolese, leadership transformation, political will and commitment, and an increase in institutional capacity and capability.

Use of locally available human resources

DRC's universities and colleges produce thousands of graduates every year. Some have completed their academic studies in fields such as medicine, civil engineering, mechanical engineering, building, mining, electrical engineering, economic sciences, and other critical disciplines. However, when it comes to employment in government-funded projects in sectors such as road building, electrification, medicine, and mining, to name just a few, the contract is given to foreign companies that will bring their own personnel from abroad, such as China and Europe. Yet most of these duties would have been well discharged by the existing local human resources and companies at low cost. While expatriates can perform high standard duties, contracting local companies can be competitively and comparatively cost-effective. Contracting local companies contributes to job creation, poverty alleviation, and a high standard of living for the local people and ultimately contributes to national economic development through taxation and trickle-down effects. The trickle-down effect is the diffusion of economic gains from the wealthy to the poor when the economy expands. Singapore can serve as a good example among several countries in the world because it has experienced continuous economic growth during the last three decades.

Furthermore, the Congolese need to develop a culture of hard work and avoid shifting the burden. For example, Americans work 24-7, and this has contributed to the prosperity of hardworking individuals and the entire nation. Americans believe in independence, competition, possibilities, diversity, and equal opportunity. If we genuinely want to take off and achieve the stage of mass production in the DRC, we need to shun a culture of laziness and hoping to reap where one did not sow. If a local company is offered a contract, it must deliver results within the budget, scope, and time limit in a transparent and accountable manner.

Meanwhile, many Congolese still believe that the root causes of their problems are colonial administration, Western imperialism, and rushed independence from Belgium. Imperialism is defined as a policy or ideology of extending the rule over peoples and other countries in order to extend political and economic access, power, and control, through employing hard power, especially military force, but also soft power. Its history states that the progress of the DRC was and still is hindered by the imperialism. Therefore, most Congolese have put too much faith in Western powers, hoping they will change their systems and come back to their rescue and salvation. This is totally wrong. We cannot change the past, but we can change our current mindset and work hard to solve our own problems without shifting the burden to outsiders. While problem-solving requires global intervention, Congolese need to learn to solve their own problems without depending too much on outsiders. Americans solve their own problems among themselves, and so do Europeans. Why should Congolese continue to shift the burden? The culture of dependence must be avoided at all costs. We need to develop partnerships that promote peace and security, interdependence, regional and international trade, science, technological development, innovation, and exchange of knowledge. This must include capacity building, joint ventures, and mutually beneficial regional and international cooperation for development.

Moreover, Congolese need to continue nurturing and preserving positive values of respecting elders and those in authority, especially government leaders. Patrice Lumumba was killed just a few months after his election as prime minister of the Congo. Mobutu died in exile. Laurent Kabila was killed in office.

This problem is not limited to the DRC alone. On October 20, 2011, Colonel Muammar al-Gaddafi, a former Libyan president was killed in Libya while the African Union leaders were just watching. The African Union (AU) is the highest continental body, consisting of the fifty-five member states that make up the countries of the African continent. It was officially launched in 2002 as a successor to the Organization of African Unity (OAU, 1963–1999).

According to the African Union website (https://au.int/en/au-nutshell), the main objectives of the OAU were, inter alia, to rid the continent of the remaining vestiges of colonization and apartheid, to promote unity and solidarity among African states, to coordinate and intensify cooperation for development, to safeguard the sovereignty and territorial integrity of member states, and to promote international cooperation within the framework of the United Nations.

However, many Africans have lost trust in the ability and capabilities of the African Union. They view it as a simple leadership club, as it has failed to effectively bring solutions to most African problems. The AU failed to intervene in the Libyan crisis. In addition, the AU is largely dependent on external donors for funding. This exposes its weaknesses and makes it irrelevant in providing African solutions to African problems.

Traditionally, the highest African values are solidarity, interdependence, and being our own brothers' keepers. If the AU leaders were truly Pan-African and united, Libya would not have been destroyed and the former president Gaddafi would not have been killed in a shameful and barbaric manner. Gaddafi was a great and transformational leader, not only for the people of Libya but also for all Africa. There is a need for the AU to restore its traditional values and regain its position as the highest intergovernmental institution in Africa, with robust ability and capabilities to provide African solutions to African problems and the ability to fund its activities through contributions from the fifty-five member countries.

To address the crisis, a multi-state NATO -led coalition began a military intervention in Libya, to implement United Nations Security Council Resolution 1973. This was in response to events during the First Libyan Civil War. NATO operation started on March 19, 2011. The intervention by the North Atlantic Treaty Organization (NATO) was probably because the African nations failed to intervene. NATO, also called the North Atlantic Alliance, is an intergovernmental military alliance between thirty European and North American countries. The organization implements the North Atlantic Treaty that was signed on April 4, 1949.

Nevertheless, several reports have confirmed that ten years after the assassination of Gaddafi, Libya has remains trapped in a spiral of violence involving armed groups, sectarian and ethnic groups, and external interference, which has led the country into absolute chaos. Thousands of Libyans have been sinking in boats, found dead on shores, and others had made it to Europe, seeking asylum, jobs, and a better life. Yet all of this was available and accessible to them in their own country (Libya) during the Muhammad Gaddafi leadership era. There is need to confess and repent our horrible sins of political intolerance and assassination that still characterize most African countries. This will require the critical components of building and developing a culture of abundance mindset; effective management of resources; and celebrating different ways of thinking, political ideologies, and opinions without recourse to violence.

The maintenance of good relationships between predecessors and successors is vital as well. We need a constructive and unifying leadership style. This wisdom and level of thinking must be desired and practiced by every civilized person because that may significantly contribute to the sustainable peace, security, and development in the DRC and Africa as a continent. The Congolese and Africans at large need to create policies, educational programs, and a legal framework that favors unity, tolerance, preservation, and celebration of our leaders' legacies, patriotism, and loyalty.

There is a need to create national eldership offices that will provide room and support to retired political leaders and encourage them to peacefully retire from politics but continue to serve as elders, mentors, and national consultants; political sciences professors; and authors of books after their departure from political offices. The predecessors must create an enabling environment but should not hinder the leadership, authority, power, and development programs of their successors. For instance, despite his weaknesses and shortfalls, Joseph Kabila needs to be celebrated and respected for all the great things he accomplished in the DRC during his nineteen years as the DRC's president. However, he should not interfere with or hinder the authority, power, and development programs of Félix Tshisekedi, his successor.

We must learn from the succession story of John the Baptist and Jesus Christ recorded in the Bible. John the Baptist said, "He must become greater and greater, and I must become less and less" (John 3:30 NLT). In the same way, Jesus said, "I tell you, of all who have ever lived, none is greater than John. Yet even the least person in the Kingdom of God is greater than he is!" (Luke 7:28 NLT). Our predecessors and successors in governmental leadership and any other type of organization and institution need to develop this kind of wisdom and mindset. We need each other. Together we can accomplish more.

Call for Africans to preserve and advance Joseph Magufuli's legacy

Joseph Magufuli was a Tanzanian political and Christian leader par excellence. He served as the fifth president of Tanzania from 2015 until his death in 2021. Unlike many African leaders who are characterized by greed and corruption, President Magufuli reduced his own salary from US$15,000 to US$4,000 per month. He had a lion's heart with zero tolerance of corruption.

In December 2015, he reduced public spending by downsizing his cabinet from thirty to nineteen to help cut down costs. Also, he suspended the country's Independence Day celebrations for 2015 and favored a national cleanup campaign to assist in reducing the spread of cholera and other diseases. He personally participated in the cleanup efforts.

His government invested heavily in electrification, road infrastructure, and industrial development and manufacturing, which contributed to economic growth. Also, his government invested in the building and upgrading of schools, hospitals, and health centers. He introduced a free education program for elementary schools up to high schools. In addition, he introduced a phenomenally successful anti-corruption policy and was able to implement most of his government projects and programs without depending on external funding. During his term of office, Tanzania recorded a high economic growth rate, which contributed to poverty alleviation and a high standard of living among Tanzanians.

Magufuli sacrificed his life to economically empower the poor in his country without dependence on external aid. This was a great demonstration that Africa is not poor. I believe that, what makes our continent poor is corruption, poor political leadership, and ill public policy, as well as, deliberate, unjust, international institutions and global political systems and ideologies that make rules and laws, institute policy programs, create standards, diffuse norms, establish agendas, decide on legal disputes, and monitor and evaluate outcomes. Therefore, the world's economic matters, namely international financial and trade institutions, are still largely controlled by the superpowers. There is need to address this problem by promoting cooperation for mutual and equal benefits.

Through Magufuli's leadership, Tanzania was moving toward becoming one of the leading prosperous countries in Africa. He will be remembered as the leader who trusted God despite the COVID-19 pandemic, pressure, and criticisms. He fought the good fight. He has finished the race. He was a great model of a true, transformational Christian leader. A transformational leader inspires positive change in followers. He or she is usually energetic, enthusiastic, and passionate. This kind of leader is usually concerned and involved in the process; and he or she focuses on helping every member of the group and society achieve their God-given dreams.

I listened to one of Magufuli's video clips. He said, "My calling is to help all Tanzanians put their trust in God." This is extremely critical because most people have forgotten that we are visitors in this world. Having a leader who lives out his faith by setting an example and who was not ashamed of spreading the gospel of Christ in a country where Islam was practiced by 35 percent of the population was incredible.

Magufuli has left an outstanding legacy of trusting God in word and action. His legacy needs to be protected and emulated by every responsible citizen and leader in Africa and beyond. We need to continue trusting the living God and serve each other in love. We need good political and religious leaders. Also, we need enabling government policies and education systems that will positively transform the mindsets of Africans and promote a culture of hardworking self-sufficiency and an abundance mindset. Magufuli's legacy needs to be included in the education system and taught to every African. Magufuli was a human being, which means he had weaknesses and failures. But I am calling on us to emulate his positive achievements and protect his legacy.

Take advantage of the critical mass in diaspora

Some African countries, such as Zimbabwe, have crafted policies that allow their citizens living in diaspora to invest in their countries of origin. The government allows them to import capital goods, such as tractors and farm implements, vehicles for public transportation, and construction equipment and materials at less than 10 percent of the costs for the purchased equipment and goods and sometimes duty free. The DRC authorities need to embrace this model, as it contributes to national development.

Moreover, the government needs to create stimulus packages, enabling policies and an environment that can allow the DRC nationals in diaspora, including those who are naturalized in other countries such as the United States of America to create businesses and make investments that support development initiatives in their country of origin.

Foreigners should also be allowed to create mutually beneficial businesses in the DRC. Business registration and operation permits application should be made easy. The business registration process and decision should not take more than three months. Work and business permits should be obtainable in a transparent manner that is free from bribery or any other corrupt means.

Livelihood opportunities for refugee youth in Tongogara Refugee Camp

This section explains the various livelihood opportunities available to refugee youth in Tongogara Camp. It will examine opportunities for wage-earning employment, self-employment, and small business ventures, as well as possibilities in agriculture, and rearing of livestock.

Youth is defined as a period of transition from the dependence of childhood to adult independence. That is why, as a category, youth is more fluid than other fixed age groups. Yet, age is the easiest way to define this group, particularly in relation to education and employment, as "youth" often refers to a person between the ages of leaving compulsory education and finding one's first job. The United Nations, for statistical purposes, defines those persons between the ages of fifteen and twenty-four as youth, without prejudice to other definitions by member states. The United States of America defines youth as those under twenty-five years old in three stages—early adolescence (under fourteen), middle adolescence (fifteen to seventeen), and late adolescence and early adulthood (eighteen to twenty-four). In Zimbabwe, youth are defined as person between fifteen and thirty-five years of age. This age range is stipulated in the Constitution of Zimbabwe and is also in line with the African continent's definition of youth as defined in the African Youth Charter. In this book, the definition of youth is between the age of fifteen and thirty-five years old.

Wage-earning employment for refugee youth

According to the World Bank (2021), starting salary in Zimbabwe was reported at US$35,725 in 2000. This amount has since declined due to decades of economic and political challenges. Presently, civil servants in Zimbabwe are among the lowest paid in Africa.

In 2014, research established that a total of fourteen refugees were employed in the education departments in preschool, primary, and secondary schools and for language lessons in Tongogara Camp. The researcher had an opportunity to speak to some of the refugees who are currently employed as teachers and asked them about the salary they earn per month. They revealed that the highest paid full-time refugee teacher receives only $100 per month. This amount is far below the minimum salary for the least paid teacher in Zimbabwe.

One of the refugee teachers said, "Although, we [refugee teachers] are lowly paid, we spend equal teaching hours at school just like other local teachers whose salaries are much higher than what we get. We have equal qualifications with other local or Zimbabwean teachers and perform our duties very well. For example, you will be teaching thirteen classes, and every class you teach [is] thirty minutes twice a week. However, the fact that we are refugees, we have been victimized and given lower salaries, which is not sufficient for us to sustain our personal and family basic needs" (interview with a refugee teacher in Tongogara Camp on March 29, 2014). This situation undermines the livelihood sustainability of these civil servant refugees working as teachers because they are underpaid. Also, low salaries have contributed to low self-esteem and undermine the possibility of these underpaid workers fulfilling their self-actualization needs. On the other side, the government of Zimbabwe has recently emphasized, "The least-paid civil servant will this month get at least US$500 as their salary increment, backdated to January 1, 2014" (*Herald*, 2014, 1).

The education officer at the Department of Social Welfare in the office of Commissioner for Refugees, who was interviewed by the researcher in Harare said, "Teachers from refugee community are not government employees. They are just volunteers and what they get on monthly basis is just a token of appreciation and not a salary. The US$100 they get on a monthly basis come from an arrangement between the Ministry of Labor and Social Welfare and UNHCR" (interview with social welfare education officer in the Office of Commissioner for Refugees, April 28, 2014).

Nevertheless, the researcher is of the opinion that, although the Department of Social Welfare and UNHCR considers these teachers volunteers, they are working full-time and have been there for many years. Therefore, there is a need to allow them to be registered with the Ministry of Education, sign employment contracts, and receive remuneration equal to that of other teachers with similar qualifications.

Due to high-rocketing inflation, wages for teachers in Zimbabwe decreased every month. As a result, educators demanded US dollar wages or the Zimbabwean dollar equivalent. In November 2020, the Zimbabwe government ignored their demands, but it increased the educators' salaries by 40 percent. Thus, a teacher now earns Z$18,000, equivalent to US$180 per month. The current situation is an indication that Zimbabwe is experiencing its own economic problems that also negatively impacts refugees who are serving in the teaching industry in Zimbabwe. Traditionally, Zimbabweans are hospitable, and they care for refugees. But the economic situation in the country is worsening. Additionally, despite their courage and hard work, many refugee youths in Zimbabwe will not achieve self-sufficiency due to low salaries, limited employment possibilities, and prevailing macroeconomic and political challenges.

According to the National Education Association (2009), the average salary for a teacher in the United States is US$60,477, and starting salaries are often below US$40,000. In the State of Texas, the average state salary was US$53,335 in the 2017/18 school year. The United States economy and education industry is growing. This country needs extra labor force not just in the education but in other sectors. These possibilities are not available to refugees in Zimbabwe and many other African countries that are currently hosting refugees in refugee camps. There is need for Americans to support President Biden's new executive order on refugee resettlement. This will contribute to addressing the plight of refugees. The refugee resettlement program is a blessing not only to the refugees but also to American people. Refugees make significant contributions to the American economy through hard work, creativity, innovation, and payment of taxes. They also bring in diverse cultural values that make America a multicultural nation.

High rate of educated and qualified unemployed youths

In 2014, research findings established that more than one thousand youth from the DRC, Rwanda, Burundi, Ivory Coast, and Ethiopia residing in Tongogara Camp have qualifications ranging from secondary and postsecondary to university degrees but are not employed. This number must have doubled by 2020 because the number of refugee arrivals in Tongogara increased from 7,892 in 2014 to 14,300 in 2020. A group of elders and country representative committee leaders at Tongogara Camp told the researcher, "We have qualified refugees including medical doctors and nurses in this camp, but they are not working because the temporary residence permit given does not allow asylum seekers and refugees to work in Zimbabwe. A few lucky refugees who are working in libraries and other places within the camp are just considered volunteers at Jesuit Refugee Service, Child Help Line, Christian Care. Some serve as interpreters, and their monthly salaries ranges from US$60 to US$80 per person per month," (interview with elders and country representatives, March 28, 2014).

This policy and low salaries given to refugees undermine their ability to achieve self-reliance. As a result, most refugees are forced to depend on monthly food aid provided by Christian Care through UNHCR funding. UNHCR officials who were interviewed by the researcher on refugee youth unemployment issue revealed:

> There is a strict policy and reservations on issue to do with refugee employment in Zimbabwe ... Refugees are allowed to work on condition that you get work permit like any other foreigner in Zimbabwe. The practice is more of protecting Zimbabweans. You cannot get a work permit for an ordinary job unless you are an expert. This is the practice of refugee encampment that affects their right to employment. This situation is also worsened by the fact that Zimbabwe's economic downturn has resulted in high unemployment and poverty among the local population. The few jobs available are reserved for Zimbabwean citizens. To my knowledge, only three refugees are gainfully employed in Zimbabwe, two are medical doctors and one lawyer is working in the attorney general's office. However, quite a good number of refugees are engaged in small jobs such as commuter omnibuses, tuck shops, and hair salons through self-employment without legal papers.

They end up being harassed and targeted by the police because the issue of accessing employment without work permit is strictly illegal in term of the law. (Interview with the UNHCR protection and program officers in Tongogara Camp, March 31, 2014)

Expressing a similar view, Mr. Mukaro, the commissioner for refugees who was interviewed by the researcher in Harare had this to say:

Employment in Zimbabwe is a problem for both locals and refugees. The policies regarding refugee employment in Zimbabwe are not favorable, in the sense that we do not regard refugees as local but as foreigners. Therefore, they should get work permits, and not every youth refugee can be given a work permit. They are given only to experts in liberal professions such as medical doctors, nurses, lawyers, and teachers. When they qualify, they do not use such qualifications in Zimbabwe, but they would use the knowledge when they go back to their home countries or when they are resettled elsewhere. (Interview with the commissioner for refugees, April 22, 2014)

Conversely, Article 17(1) and 18 of the 1951 United Nations Refugee Convention provide for the right to engage in wage-earning employment or self-employment. Wage-earning and self-employment opportunities play a critical role in enabling youth refugees to pursue productive livelihoods that lead to self-reliance. The refugee convention guarantees refugees "the most favorable treatment" possible, meaning that they must be treated as other foreign nationals in different circumstances.

The researcher's view is that the unemployment situation among youth refugees is aggravated by the economic downturn in Zimbabwe. This view was also expressed by Mr. Zengeya, who was the camp administrator during the time when the research was conducted. He said, "Zimbabweans with master's degrees are currently selling vegetables on the street." His statement emphasized the scarcity of formal employment among well-educated local Zimbabweans in their own country. Therefore, there are extremely limited opportunities for refugees to access formal employment in Zimbabwe due to the poor macroeconomic situation prevailing in the country.

Most of these refuges cannot voluntarily return to their home countries because of war and insecurity. As a result, they are living is a state of hopelessness. I strongly believe that the United States of America and other developed countries have the capacity to help the hopeless and vulnerable refugees through refugee resettlement programs and by promoting sustainable peace in war-affected countries.

Self-Employment

The education officer at the camp said that there are about 150 self-employed refugees throughout Zimbabwe. Out of this number 30 to 50 are living in Tongogara Refugee Camp. This was evidenced by the presence of a few tuck shops, two beer halls, and a few commuter omnibuses that are run mainly by youth refugees from Rwanda and Burundi, as observed by the researcher.

On the other hand, the researcher established that, due to the high unemployment experienced in Tongogara Camp, some youth refugees who used to live in Tongogara Camp have relocated to Harare. The researcher managed to visit Mbare Musika (public market for fresh vegetables and other farm produce) and found a total of twenty youth refugees operating small businesses such as tuck shops and barber shops. Upon being asked how they got the capital to start these small businesses, the majority revealed that they'd received remittances from family members and friends living overseas. It was also established that some refugees, especially from Rwanda, owned a few omnibuses operating in different routes around the Harare. Most drivers and conductors of these minibuses were Zimbabwean citizens. Personally, I was an owner of an eighteen-seat minibus that operated on the Marlborough city center route in Harare for over ten years. My employees, namely the bus driver and conductor, were both Zimbabwean citizens.

With the current macroeconomic challenges and the lockdown due to the COVID-19 pandemic, most of the above-named projects are no longer functional. This has pushed innovative, creative, self-employed refugee youths to unemployment and a state of abject poverty.

Vocational training initiatives as a strategy for sustainable livelihoods

Jesuit Refugee Service, Silveira House, and NODED have introduced a variety of vocational training in areas such as cosmetology, hairdressing, dressmaking, building, computer training, welding, plumbing, electronics, fencing, carpentry, auto mechanics, and catering. This short-term vocational training was meant to contribute to employment creation and supplement household incomes among the refugee community.

Tendai Makoni, JRS National Coordinator said, "The food basket for refugees has been reduced and this is what prompted JRS to undertake a vocational training program to empower refugees to be self-reliant. So far, we have trained 160 youth in our first intake, and we are now registering a new group" (interview with Tendai Makoni, JRS National Coordinator, April 27, 2014).

The success of this project was largely dependent on both the ability of trainees to get operational support after their graduation and the existence of reliable markets for their commodities. With both, they could effectively practice the knowledge gained and create self-sustaining employment. Unfortunately, the agencies providing refugee services are underfunded and cannot provide operational support to the graduates. The Zimbabwean economy is also down, resulting in low demand and/or market for the commodities produced by them. Funding for UNHCR and other agencies providing services to refugees' overseas needs to be increased to capacitate their efforts to help refugees help themselves in their countries of asylum.

Monthly food distribution

Due to budgetary constraints, the UNCHR canceled giving money (US$13), which was provided as a monthly food basket per person and resumed monthly food handouts distribution. Most refugees were grateful for the food assistance, but the quantity of food provided to them is not enough to feed one person for two weeks. As such, most refugees are reduced to one meal per two days. Speaking to this situation, one of the respondents said, "While we are not able to find jobs, the food basket we receive on monthly basis is not sufficient, not given on a regular basis, and has been further reduced. This situation has increased our vulnerability, dependence, poverty, and suffering. Also, it is fueling promiscuous behavior and sexually transmitted diseases among young people in Tongogara Refugee Camp" (Zoom conference interview respondent, January 2021).

According to Maslow's hierarchy of needs, food is an element of physiological needs for human survival. Hunger and malnutrition may lead to disease and death. This situation forced many refugees, especially women, to engage in extramarital affairs for survival. Young girls were forced into early marriage, and many boys and men moved to South Africa and other neighboring countries due to food shortages and hunger experienced in the Tongogara Camp.

Life in refugee camps is hard, and refugees who have lived in refugee camps for over five years develop a dependency syndrome, low self-esteem, and low self-confidence, which reduces them to the state of beggars. Most refugees in the camp come to think more about what they can receive from UNHCR and other humanitarian agencies and less about what they can do for themselves and their families because there are limited opportunities for them to achieve their personal and family dreams.

Refugees in the Tongogara Camp are surviving on food handouts equivalent to less than $13 per month. Meanwhile, they could make this amount of money or more per hour on their own by working for companies or creating their own jobs here in the United States and in other developed countries. Therefore, I am advocating for a rapid increase of refugee family arrivals through the United States and United Nations refugee resettlement programs. Increasing the capacity and capabilities of this humanitarian service and program will restore self-confidence and dignity to vulnerable refugees.

I am appealing to the United States president; to federal and state government leaders and legislators; to churches, civil society organizations, and business leaders; and to all Americans to welcome people who were forced to leave their home countries and habitual residence due to fear of persecution, war, and conflict. Welcoming strangers is an instruction from God. For example, Jesus said:

> For I was hungry, and you gave me something to eat, I was thirsty, and you gave me something to drink, I was a stranger and you invited me in. I needed clothes and you

clothed me, I was sick, and you looked after me, I was in prison and you came to visit me. Then the righteous will answer him, "Lord, when did we see you hungry and feed you, or thirsty and give you something to drink? When did we see you a stranger and invite you in, or needing clothes and clothe you? When did we see you sick or in prison and go to visit you?" The King will reply, "Truly I tell you, whatever you did for one of the least of these brothers and sisters of mine, you did for me." (Matthew 25:35–40)

Agriculture

The researcher also established that, by the end of 2013, UNHCR provided small plots, seeds, and fertilizer to 325 refugee households, who managed to grow some maize to supplement their food ration. This is a particularly good initiative and needs to be expanded for all the people in the camp so that they can supplement their monthly food ration. The UNHCR and other agencies involved in providing refugee services need to be well funded to enable them to effectively assist refugees in growing their own food to supplement the monthly food ration assistance in the amount of US$13. In addition, this amount is not sufficient and needs to be increased to at least US$50 to US$100 per person per month. This will require an increase in funding of the UNCHR and other agencies providing refugee services overseas. Refugees should be assisted to move from dependency to self-sufficiency.

Other livelihood projects undertaken by youth refugees

In 2014, a limited number of refugee youth were involved in various activities, ranging from brick molding to selling food stuffs, clothing, and cattle as a strategy to supplement their food rations and create income. Some of these activities have been supported by various nongovernmental organizations. For example, Aziza Abemba, executive director of Women's Self-Promotion Movement (WSPM), said, "Our organization has provided goats to fifty refugee households in Tongogara camp as a contribution to their income-generation strategies to supplement their food baskets and assist in meeting other nonfood needs for their households. We provided two female goats to each household. WSPM also provides leadership training for women and girls to help them gain self-confidence, self-esteem, and self-determination. Our capacity building program also helps women and girl refugees to understand their rights and exercise them" (interview with WSPM director, April 4, 2014).

WSPM successfully registered an international office in Texas, United State of America. WSPM's leadership, women's human rights and political participation, economic empowerment programs, micro- ending, and employment skills training serve poor and disenfranchised women in Zimbabwe, Zambia, Tanzania, and the Democratic Republic of the Congo (DRC), including widows, single heads of households, and refugee women and girls. The organization is currently seeking to build partnership with individuals and organizations in the United States and around the world to empower women and refugees in Africa and other parts of the global south. Refugee youth need to be supported to venture in self-employment activities to assist them to help themselves.

Socioeconomic challenges and impact on youths

In a group discussion conducted with ten women and girls, it was established that most youth refugees (about 97 percent) are currently unemployed and living below the poverty datum line with no hope for a better future. It was also established that due to socioeconomic and household food insecurity challenges, many minor girls are getting involved in promiscuous behavior and sexual transactions to supplement their household food ration. In addition, inability to access wage-earning employment and accommodation challenges have prompted many parents—in urgent need of cash from bride price (lobola) to provide for basic household needs—to force their minor girls to engage in early marriages. Forced marriage and gender discrimination perpetuates feminization of poverty and are impediments to the achievement of gender equality and empowerment of women.

During the group discussion, some of the young women and men were open to discussing the existence of sexually transmitted diseases among youths, which is fueled by the promiscuous behaviors attributed to poverty and unemployment. They tried to seek medical attention and/or assistance in the camp, but there was not enough medication. These groups need to be helped through capacity building programs that will help them venture into income-generating activities in refugee camps while seeking durable solutions through refugee resettlement programs or voluntary repatriation when the security situation stabilizes in their home countries.

Unfavorable climatic conditions and location of refugee camps

Climatic conditions and soil types in many refugee camps are not suitable for refugees' sustainable livelihoods. This is the case in the Tongogara Refugee Camp in Zimbabwe. A study conducted in the camp by a previous researcher revealed the following challenges are being experienced due to its unfavorable climatic and soil conditions: "It is in the rain shadow area of Chimanimani Mountains, as a result, the region does not benefit from rains that blow inland from the Indian Ocean. Thus, the ground in the area is very dry and not suitable for agricultural activities, making it difficult for refugees to farm. The temperatures in the region are remarkably high. The estimated average temperatures are as high as 35 and 38 degrees Celsius. The region and the camp also are prone to flooding, as it is situated downstream from local rivers" (Badibanga 2010, 26).

Based on Badibanga's description and what has been discussed in preceding chapters, it is clear that many refugee settlements are located in unfriendly environments that make it difficult for youth refugees to be productive. Kakuma Refugee Camp is a desert, and Tongogara is also a dry place with very harsh weather and a lack of suitable land for productive farming activities. As a result, some youth refugees take their chances on crossing borders to reach South Africa in search of greener pastures and return only when the registration exercise begins.

Looking back at the history of refugee encampment, one can associate it with the children of Israel when they went to Egypt. They were relocated in Goshen, a fertile area, which led them to be productive and feed themselves and help in growing the Egyptian economy. This means, if refugees in contemporary refugee camps were in fertile areas, they too could be productive and feed themselves. Unfortunately, the current reality is likely to produce a community of beggars and economic dependents—people who are miserable due to the fact that they are being settled in unproductive places, where productive farming opportunities are a challenge and access to wage earning and self-employment opportunities are scarce, leading to household food and income insecurity and abject poverty.

In 2014, a humanitarian agency named Christian Care allocated small plots to some refugee households and helped them to invest in market gardening. This was a positive development. But this program is no longer functional because of financial or budgeting constraints. Christian Care is no longer operating in the Tongogara Refugee Camp.

These farming initiatives must be renewed within the camp. And so must vocational training by JRS and NODED and WSPM's interventions and activities. Resuming, supporting, and expanding all of these programs will benefit all refugees in the camp.

On the other hand, I am appealing to developed countries such as the United States of America, Australia, Canada, and European countries to assist the abandoned, abundant labor force available in refugee camps in Africa and other countries of the world by providing humanitarian support and increasing and speeding up their resettlement programs. Also, they should increase financial support to the United Nations High Commissioner for Refugees (UNHCR) and other humanitarian agencies involved in helping refugees in the refugee camps and urban refugees around the world. Furthermore, agencies that provide refugee resettlement and capacity building services for refugees' successful integration after their arrival in developed countries including the United States need to be well supported financially by local and federal governments. Also, individuals, churches, foundations, and corporations need to provide donations and grants to support agencies involved in refugee resettlement and empowerment programs. Most importantly, there a is need for world leaders, including our African leaders, to address the root causes of conflict, wars, and instability. We need to work together to promote sustainable peace and development in countries affected by wars. This will help most refugees return home and rebuild their lives in their home countries.

Educational opportunities

Education is recognized as the cornerstone for development and critical strategy for youth empowerment. Article 22 of the 1951 Convention

Relating to the Status of Refugees states that signatory states "shall accord to refugees the same treatment as is accorded to nationals with respect to elementary education ... [and] treatment as favorable as possible ... with respect to education other than elementary education" (UNHCR 2010). Zimbabwe is a signatory to the 1951 Convention Relating to the Status of Refugees, its 1967 Protocol, and the 1969 OAU Convention on Specific Problems of Refugees in Africa.

Primary school education

According to a 2021 World Vision report, Tongogara Refugee Camp boasts the largest primary and secondary schools in Zimbabwe, with more than 3,600 and 2,000 students, respectively. In other words, there is one primary school located about two kilometers away from the camp's residential area called Tongogara Primary School. In 2014, Tongogara Primary School had a total of 1,444 students. The number of students increased to 3,600, and over 80 percent of the pupils are refugee children. Some of the pupils who participated in a focus group discussion in 2014 informed me of how they felt about their schooling. One explained, "We value education because it can help us to have a better future; therefore, we take it seriously and we are trying our best" (group discussion respondent from Tongogara Primary School, March 28 2014). These students, most of whom were from twelve to thirteen years old, already had a clear understanding of the importance of education and how it could contribute to shaping their future.

Mr. John the school Deputy Head said, "Some of the students from the camp are performing very well and are uplifting the standard of the school. They are also performing well in art and sport. All the awards medals are won by students from the camp. If they were to be sent back today, the standard of this school is likely to go down because most local [Zimbabwean] students are far behind, and this may negatively affect the reputation and standard of this school if all refugees were to be sent back to their home countries (interview with the deputy headmaster at Tongogara Primary School, March 28, 2014).

This situation is a demonstration that, despite the language barrier, youths from refugee backgrounds exhibit high levels of strength, resilience, and resourcefulness and are an untapped resource that can be developed and equipped to become meaningful assets and resource persons. This can also be explained by the fact that the standard of education in Zimbabwe is higher than that of some other African countries.

Shortage of classrooms at Tongogara Primary School

The current report has established that the number of students at Tongogara Primary School has increased from 1,444 (in 2014) to 3,600 (as of December 2020). Most of these new classes are conducted under the trees. Unfortunately, the weather in the Tongogara area is extremely hot and windy. Children and teachers cannot concentrate outside. This situation has resulted in poor performance and dropouts among students.

In 2014, research established that the school was facing some challenges that were affecting the school standards and performance of students. One of the challenges noted was the shortage of classrooms, which was forcing almost half of students to attend classes under trees. Both the school deputy head and camp administrator were concerned, noting, "Tongogara Primary School has currently twenty-nine classes with only fifteen classrooms. This is forcing fourteen teachers and classes to be conducted under trees and in the open air" (interview with Deputy headmaster and camp administrator, March 28 and April 2, 2014).

Expressing a similar view on and experience of the poor-quality education for refugees elsewhere, Peterson (2011) an expert in UNHCR policy and development service states that the lack of high quality and protective education for refugees stands in the way of meeting goals of education for all goals, of achieving durable solutions, and of sustainable development and reconstruction of home and host countries. The fact is that the number of refugee students have continued to increase; there is need for UNHCR to build new blocks at the primary and secondary schools in Tongogara to address the crisis of classroom shortage. Quality and suitable education is necessary for youth refugee empowerment. Given technological development, the building of computer labs and introduction of computer lessons and practice for refugee pupils at primary and secondary schools in the Tongogara Refugee Camp is especially important. UNHCR, the government of Zimbabwe, and other local and international well-wishers and donors must support this need.

There is need for the Ministry of Labor and Social Welfare through the office of Commissioner for Refugees to educate, engage, and sign a memorandum of understanding and binding policy with the Ministry of Education to allow refugees to pay school fees according to what is paid by Zimbabweans.

Hunger and uniform shortage

One of the students who participated in the focus group discussion talked about the plight of fellow students:

> Due to our household food insecurity, many of us are going
> to school without taking breakfast. As a result, many of us
> fall hungry in class and fail to concentrate on our studies,
> and others ended up in nearby maize field where they are
> caught stealing maize from other people's fields. In addition,
> many of us come to school without shoes and with very dirty
> and torn uniforms. This is since we only receive one set of
> uniform, that is a shirt and short for a boy and one dress for a
> girl without shoes for an irregular period of one to two years
> from UNHCR through the Department of Social Welfare.
> (focus group discussion respondent, March 28, 2014)

This situation undermines children's ability to study properly, as they are coming to school with empty stomachs. It also affects their hygiene, as they walk four kilometers on foot every day on dusty roads without proper school shoes. And only one uniform for a period of one to two years is not good enough, considering the heat and cold weather that affect them.

Secondary school education

The research established that there is one secondary school, which is called St. Michael's Tongogara Secondary School. This school is located about five hundred meters away from Tongogara Camp's residential area next to a sports ground. In 2014, there were 389 students. But there are now 2,000 students (as of December 2020). Over 1,700 are refugees and asylum seekers.

Dr. Joseph Boomenyo

Source of sponsorship for refugee students

The research established that all refugee students attending school at both Tongogara Primary School and Saint Michael's Tongogara Secondary School are sponsored by UNHCR, and the funds are disbursed through the Department of Social Welfare within the Ministry of Labor and Social Welfare.

Challenges experienced at Saint Michael's Tongogara Secondary School

The deputy headmaster for St. Michael's Secondary School said, "When a refugee family is interviewed for resettlement to go either to America or Canada, students do not take education seriously. They concentrate on resettlement and put less effort to studies. They think, if they go to the USA or Canada, the certificates from the Zimbabwean education will not be considered in the resettlement country. This situation poses a lot of challenges because most refugees end up underperforming and misbehaving. However, this behavior is changing after some refugees have realized that Zimbabwe certificates are accepted in some developed countries" (interview with deputy headmaster at St. Michael's Tongogara Secondary School, March 27, 2014).

I am pleased to mention that refugees who attended secondary and postsecondary education in their countries of asylum before relocating to a third country or country of resettlement, such as the United States, have been able to secure good employment soon after their arrival in the United States. Typical examples are Tresor Fikiri and Jean-Claude Mauridi, who have both served as case managers at Texas Refugee Services in Fort Worth, Texas. Also, children who completed their elementary school in English-speaking countries did not have difficulty adjusting to the American education system. Typical examples are my own children, who are doing very well in elementary and high schools because of having attended better schools in Harare, Zimbabwe. My sons Obed and Kijana successfully completed the twelve grades at Southwest High School in Fort Worth, Texas. They both moved to a local university where they are taking academic courses.

There is a need to increase the capacity of schools and educational institutions in refugee camps and give them priority in terms of funding to

92

enable refugee children and youth to access quality education and training while they are still living in their second country or country of asylum. Education is a cornerstone to the empowerment and self-sufficiency of refugees.

Scholarship shortage challenges

It was also established that, due to limited scholarships, many refugee students who performed well at secondary schools failed to attend postsecondary and university studies. Some refugees who came to Zimbabwe with completed secondary education qualifications and were in need of proceeding to university were also experiencing similar challenges.

UNHCR, through the Albert Einstein Germany Academic Refugee Initiative (DAFI) scholarships program in Zimbabwe, provided about ten scholarships or less each year, leaving thousands of deserving refugee youth with no opportunities to continue their education beyond high school. UNHCR and other agencies involved in refugee services need to be funded to enable them to provide scholarships to refugees. Also, most of these youth can be resettled to developed countries and given financial aid to proceed with their tertiary education. Youth access to lifelong education, especially colleges and universities, can contribute to solving refugee problems affecting our world today.

*Shortage of educational materials, lack of computer/
internet facilities, and language barrier*

It was established that there is a shortage of books and other updated educational materials at both the primary and secondary schools in Tongogara. There is a need for building a resource library to contribute to the delivery of quality education that can also improve the passing rate at these schools.

The researcher established that there was not even one computer laboratory at either of the schools. However, given the rapid change in education systems and the importance of information, and communication technology, there is an urgent need for theoretical and practical computer and internet lessons, as well as a library whereby students can conduct research using internet search engines and communicate with one another through e-mail. Also, it was established that most students from the refugee community who register at Tongogara Primary School and St. Michael's Secondary School are from French-speaking countries, but the education system in Zimbabwe is conducted in Shona and English. This situation has resulted in some of the refugee students having serious problems understanding lessons, often leading to students dropping out due to language constraints.

Refugee Empowerment Network, a 501(c)(3) based in Texas, is seeking to partner with individuals, schools, colleges, universities, churches, and other donor organizations to secure new and used (but working) computers and funding. Funds will be used to implement computer training centers and ESL programs for refugees living in refugee camps in Africa and to provide capacity-building programs and services to resettled refugees in Fort Worth, Texas, and other cities in the United States.

Urban refugees denied access to scholarships

There is no free education in most African countries. As such, school-going children and youth refugees living in urban areas, especially in Harare, are not given sponsorships, except a few lucky students who receive funds for forms four to six (equivalent of grades ten to twelve). The refugee educational policy states that refugees applying for scholarships must be staying in Tongogara Camp, yet the camp is now overcrowded beyond capacity. This situation undermines urban refugee policy and robs many young urban refugees of their future, as most parents have no sufficient income to pay for the school fees being charged in primary and secondary schools in urban areas.

In addition, due to limited scholarships, most youths who qualify to go to university end up on the streets of Harare doing nothing. Others get engaged in early marriage, which negatively affects their future. They are traumatized and hopeless. There is need for UNHCR to secure funding and help urban refugee children and youth to access scholarships and continue their education. Also, the resettlement program should prioritize urban refugees. When they are here in the United States, they can continue their education, go to work, and take care of their own needs.

Amenities and Services

Electricity and water supply in Tongogara Camp

In January 2014, the Zimbabwe Electricity Distribution Company switched off the supply of electricity to the camp because the UNHCR and refugees could not manage to pay the monthly bills. Electricity has never been restored to the camp.

A result of the lack of electricity is the loss of clean domestic water supplies in the camp. This has increased the outbreak of diarrhea and other diseases to a degree the clinic is not able to cope with. Ms. Tendai Makoni, JRS national coordinator said, "The cutting of power is bad; it really negatively affected the operation and productivity of our vocational training projects because we are now using a generator and it is not big enough to supply power needed for our operation. It is even better if power can be restored and each organization will be paying their own bills" (interview with Ms. Tendai Makoni, March 27, 2014).

I have been living in Fort Worth, Texas, since November 2017. On Sunday February 14, 2021, the state of Texas experienced one of the worst winter storms in its history. Snow began to fall on Sunday and continued until Thursday, February 18, 2021. We saw one of the worst road accidents ever recorded in American history. This accident happened on the route that I frequently use to go to church and for my daily work activities. During these few days, water and electricity supplies were cut in most areas because of the storm damage. Texas's governor declared a state of emergency because he understood the importance of water and electricity.

In contrast, officials in Zimbabwe have left this problem unresolved for over five years. Leaving 14,300 refugees without clean water and electricity for so long is not proper, considering the dilapidated health system in Zimbabwe and devastating effects of COVID-19 virus and other diseases.

The cutting of electricity and water supplies is a chronic problem experienced by several African countries, including the DRC. There is need to improve these crucial services.

Effects of power cut on refugees and environmental challenges

It was established that, due to the power cut, youths living in the camp are now exposed to wild animals, which roam during the night within the camp, especially elephants. A few months before I conducted my research work in Tongogara Camp, a young refugee from South Sudan was killed by an elephant, which had wandered astray toward the camp. A young boy from Rwanda was also viciously attacked by a crocodile when he went to play in a nearby river, just two hundred meters from Tongogara Refugee Camp.

In addition, electricity was the main source of cooking fuel for refugees. As a result, cutting down trees for charcoal and firewood has become the chief source of energy among the refugees. However, cutting down trees can have a negative impact on the environment and is legally prohibited in Zimbabwe.

It was also established that, before the electricity was cut off, some refugees could have televisions in their homes and were able to watch news and have some entertainment. However, due to the cutting of the electricity, many couples have revealed that the only remaining entertainment for them is sex and making children.

Boreholes available aren't enough to provide for household needs

While the total population residing in Tongogara Refugee Camp is currently 14,300, there are only fifteen boreholes, only ten of which are functioning. This means each borehole is catering to 1,430 people. This is not adequate, especially when social distancing is required. Therefore, some youths wake up at 3:00 a.m. to join the queue for water and only manage to get twenty liters of water at around 10:00 a.m. This situation affects the hygiene of refugees, particularly school-age children and youth.

World Vision, one of the humanitarian agencies currently working in the camp, has promised to repair and maintain the fifteen boreholes. World Vision plans to increase the number of water points to alleviate the problem.

Health and medical facilities in Tongogara Camp

The camp population is 14,300, but there is not even one medical doctor in the camp. One participant in a group discussion noted, "The few nurses available are not managing to provide quality health and medical services to refugees" (telephone interview respondent, February 19, 2021).

It was also established that language barriers are also an impediment to health and medical care. This is especially true for new arrivals from French- and

Swahili-speaking countries, some of whom, after falling sick in the camp and being transferred outside the camp, end up dying in Chipinge Hospital due to communication breakdowns between the patients and doctors.

There is need for a permanent medical doctor and multilingual nurses to save human lives in Tongogara Camp.

Policies and Legislations

The process of registering asylum seekers and refugees in Zimbabwe

The research has established that, when asylum seekers are received in Zimbabwe, they are provided with basic emergency services and facilities such as water, shelter, health care, medical services, and food, as well as burial land. The Department of Social Service in the Ministry of Labor and Social Welfare works hand in hand with the Central Intelligent Organization (CIO), national police, and the UNHCR, as well as the Immigration Department and others in the Ministry of Home Affairs to provide security to refugees. The government and its different departments and ministries play a leading role in terms of registering refugees and providing temporary residential permits, visas, and refugee identification cards. This process is carried out to facilitate the safety and security of vulnerable refugees when they enter Zimbabwe. During the registration process UNHCR provides refugees with ration cards.

At this stage, refugees also go through a screening process through various interviews with the Zimbabwe National Refugee Committee, which is composed of various members from the Commissioner for Refugees Office, the CIO, and the UNHCR. This committee has the power to accept or reject applications submitted by individual asylum seekers in Zimbabwe. When a person is accepted, the refugee is granted a refugee status, which allows him or her to stay in Zimbabwe on a temporary residential permit. When the asylum seeker is rejected, he or she is given three months to move out of Zimbabwe.

Analysis of the new constitution of Zimbabwe and refugee integration

I established that the new Constitution of Zimbabwe (2013) is people centered because it approval came out of a referendum conducted in March

2013. For example, Section 3 (e) provides for the recognition of the inherent dignity and worth of all human beings and recognition of the equality of all human beings. These are the fundamental values of this new constitution. Section 14 (1) also provides that the government of Zimbabwe should facilitate the empowerment and employment of marginalized persons, groups, and communities in Zimbabwe. Section 38 (1 and 2) provides room for integration of refugees in Zimbabwe. Although, the constitution provides for all these, the government is yet to comply with the constitutional provisions when it comes to refugees.

The camp administrator revealed that a group of refugees from Rwanda have already made an application for permanent residence to the government of Zimbabwe in terms of section 38 (2) of the new Constitution of Zimbabwe. The government of Zimbabwe has not yet given them a response. However, the Commissioner for Refugees and the camp administrator, in addition to the UNHCR protection officer, have all revealed that the Zimbabwean government does not permit permanent residence and naturalization of refugees in Zimbabwe. There is, however, a need for an application to be made to the constitutional court on that issue. This is an indication that there is a gap between legislation and policy formulation and implementation. Most policy documents sound good on paper, but there exists the challenge of implementation.

According to the International Refugee Organization (2013, 9) once an asylum seeker is granted refugee status, the person is given an opportunity to become a permanent resident and even naturalized citizen in South Africa and most Western countries, as well as Australia.

Analysis of Refugee Act chapter 4:03

The Refugee Act (chapter 4:03) is considered the legal instrument for refugee issues in Zimbabwe. Article 22 (2) provides, "The Contracting States shall accord to refugees treatment as favorable as possible, and, in any event, not less favorable than that accorded to aliens generally in the same circumstances, with respect to education other than elementary education and as regards access to studies, the recognition of foreign school certificates, diplomas and degrees, the remission of fees and charges and the award of scholarships."

Zimbabwe is one of the countries with the highest literacy rates in Africa. This explains why this country prioritizes refugee access to education, especially in Tongogara Camp, where a total of 3,600 children are currently getting a primary school education. However, students in Tongogara Camp are studying in difficult conditions as previously explained, and this undermines the quality of education provided in the camp.

In comparison to Tongogara Refugee Camp, most youth refugees living in urban areas such as Harare are not enjoying similar access to educational opportunities. As a result, most abandon studies due to lack of scholarships. Refugee encampment policy confines refugees in the camp as prerequisite for scholarships.

In addition, some youth refugees who pay for their own education are being forced by the Ministry of Education and some schools to produce study permits and pay extraterritorial fees that are much higher than what local students pay. Students with refugee status should be exempt from paying extraterritorial fees. In other words, they are supposed to pay similar amounts to local students.

In responding to this controversial issue, the commissioner for refugees said, "At one time we were successful, and all refugees could pay school fees similar to that of Zimbabweans. This problem is due to personnel changes in the Ministry of Education. We need to reengage them" (interview with the commissioner for refugees, April 22, 2014).

The research established that the DRC Diplôme D'état—national diplomas considered equivalent to a baccalaureate in France or advanced-level certificates that lead to university in Zimbabwe—are being degraded by the Zimbabwe School Examination Council. The council considers and/or translates that the DRC's advanced level diplomas are equivalent to an ordinary level certificate in Zimbabwe. This situation blocks many qualified youths from proceeding to postsecondary and university studies in Zimbabwe. However, the DRC Diplôme D'état is accepted at other universities elsewhere, including in developed countries.

Articles 18 and 19 of the Zimbabwe Refugee Act provide for access to self-employment and liberal professions.

According to Article 18, "The Contracting States shall accord to a refugee lawfully in their territory treatment as favorable as possible and, in any event, not less favorable than that accorded to aliens generally in the same circumstances, as regards the right to engage on his own account in agriculture, industry, handicrafts and commerce and to establish commercial and industrial companies."

Article 19 of the same refugee Act stipulates that:

1. Each Contracting State shall accord to refugees lawfully staying in their territory who hold diplomas recognized by the competent authorities of that State, and who are desirous of practicing a liberal profession, treatment as favorable as possible and, in any event, not less favorable than that accorded to aliens generally in the same circumstances.
2. The Contracting States shall use their best endeavors consistent with their laws and constitutions to secure the settlement of such refugees in the territories, other than the metropolitan territory, for whose international relations they are responsible. (Zimbabwe Refugee Act, chapter 4:03 1983)

Permanent residence and naturalization of refugees and the implication for youths' potential to achieve sustainable livelihoods

Many countries that are signatories to the 1951 Refugee Convention provide opportunities for permanent residence and naturalization of refugees in their countries to facilitate their local integration. By so doing, they enable refugees to become socially, culturally, and economically integrated into the society. This is the case in South Africa and most developed countries, such as Australia, the United States, Sweden, Norway, and Canada.

However, the commissioner for refugees said, "Zimbabwean law does not permit naturalization of refugees in this country" (interview with commissioner for refugees in Harare, April 22, 2014). He also added that "children of refugees born in Zimbabwe do not qualify for citizenship." This situation undermines livelihood sustainability for many youth refugees who have stayed in Zimbabwe for over five years. Because they are viewed as visitors, many of them cannot engage in long-term productive investments.

Analysis of Education Act chapter 25:04 and UNHCR's education policy

Zimbabwe's Education Act acknowledges the fundamental rights to education in Zimbabwe. Therefore, during the first decade of Zimbabwean independence, education was provided for free, which contributed positively to a high literacy rate in Zimbabwe. Now that education is no longer free, many local and refugee children, especially in urban areas, are dropping out due to high school fees. This situation undermines the achievement of the United Nations Sustainable Development Goals 2030. It also robs many promising children, both Zimbabweans and refugees who drop out of school due to poverty, of their future.

Peterson (2011) reported on UNHCR's Policy Development and Evaluation Service, saying:

> "Access to education for refugees is limited and uneven across regions and settings of displacement ... Enrollment in primary school is only 76% globally and drops dramatically to 36% at secondary levels. Girls are at a particular disadvantage; in eastern and the Horn of Africa, only five girls are enrolled for every ten boys. In addition, refugee education is generally of an exceptionally low quality, with ineffective indicators that measure inputs rather than outcomes. Teacher pupil ratios average as high as 1:70 and, in many situations, teachers do not have even the ten days of training that would categorize them as "trained." Available data indicate that many refugee children are learning little in schools; among Eritrean refugees in Ethiopia, less than 6% of refugee children reached benchmark reading fluency by grade 4".

This describes the reality in Tongogara Camp, where most classes at Tongogara Primary School are being conducted under trees. This jeopardizes the quality of education, as both children and teachers cannot concentrate. It results in high absenteeism and dropout rates, especially among girls, who end up engaging in early marriage or becoming pregnant and fail to reach ordinary and advanced levels in their education. The research established that there are not any computer labs where students can learn how to use computers at either the primary or secondary school in the camp.

The plight of asylum seekers and rejected refugee youth

The research also established that about half of the youth living in Tongogara Camp are of asylum seekers and rejected mostly on national security grounds. This group of youths informed the researcher of their situation. One noted, "We are not considered to benefit from UNHCR scholarships program and not allowed to participate in vocational training being conducted by JRS, Silveira House and NODED in Tongogara Refugee Camp," (interview with an asylum seeker from DRC, whose application status was rejected, March 30, 2014). This situation is undermining the achievement of sustainable development goals. There is a need to promote greater investment in youth access to educational opportunities for their protection, development, self-reliance, and empowerment needs.

Conclusion

This chapter has explained various unmet human needs identified during my scientific research conducted at the Tongogara Refugee Camp. Some needs are negotiable, and others are nonnegotiable, as they negatively affect educational and sustainable livelihood strategies for refugee youth. Both Maslow and Burton acknowledged the importance of addressing human needs and that failure to do so may result in social and political conflicts and lack of peace. The chapter also presented a few suggestions and recommendations that would contribute to finding durable solutions to the plight of refugees. The emphasis is on the need for all Americans to support President Biden's new executive order on refugee resettlement.

In our present era, the United States is the "promised land" for refugees. Let us open our hearts and our hands to receive people who were forced to leave their countries because of war, conflict, and persecution.

The following chapter explains the process of admitting refugees into the United States. It also explains why the United States is indeed the refugees' promise land.

CHAPTER 6

THE UNITED STATES OF AMERICA AS THE PROMISED LAND FOR REFUGEES

Introduction

The previous chapters explained the difficult living conditions due to limited employment and educational opportunities for refugee youth in the Tongogara Refugee Camp in Zimbabwe and other refugee camps in African countries that uphold refugee encampment policies of confinement. They demonstrate how restricting the freedom of movement of refugees and asylum seekers hinders their efforts to become self-reliant and self-sufficient. This chapter focuses on the importance of the United States of America's Refugee Resettlement Program. It explains the process of resettling refugees into the United States—from the selection process, including health and security screening to travel to refugees' arrival up to the granting of permanent residence and citizenship through naturalization. The United States Refugee Resettlement Program provides great and practical possibilities for refugees to meet their human needs and to participate in the national economic development and politics in the United States through labor, entrepreneurship, employment creation, and payment of taxes. Becoming active citizens, refugees can become a blessing to others within and outside the United States' borders.

This chapter concludes that the United States of America is the promised land for people who have experienced religious persecution and those who were forced to leave their home countries due to war, conflict, and political instability. The US Refugee Resettlement Program is an answered prayer to the plight of refugees. It is important to acknowledge that most notes included in many sections of this chapter were taken directly from the US Department of State, US Homeland Security, and the US Department of Health and Human Services, Office of Refugee Resettlement documents available on these agency's websites.

Why the United States of America is the promised land for refugees

In biblical times, the Lord said to Abram, "Go from your country, your people and your father's household to the land I will show you. I will make you into a great nation, and I will bless you; I will make your name great, and you will be a blessing. I will bless those who bless you, and whoever curses you I will curse; and all peoples on earth will be blessed through you" (Genesis 12:1–3).

In the above passage, we see Abram, whose name means "exalted father" and who is later named Abraham, meaning "the father of multitude or many nations." A native of Ur in Mesopotamia, Abram was called by God (Yahweh) to leave his native country, habitual residence, and people and journey to a new and unfamiliar land, where he would become the founder of a new nation. God promised to (1) make him into a great nation, (2) bless him and bless all those who blessed him, (3) curse whoever cursed him, (4) make his name great, and (5) make him a blessing to others.

Abram obeyed God and left his country and his people. God fulfilled his promises to Abraham by providing a land full of honey and milk for him and his offspring. The land is currently known as the land of the Hebrew nation, or Israel. Israel is in the Middle East on the Mediterranean Sea. This country is regarded by Jews, Christians, and Muslims as the biblical Holy Land. Its most holy sites are in Jerusalem. Within its Old City, the Temple Mount complex includes the Dome of the Rock shrine, the historic Western Wall, Al-Aqsa Mosque, and the Church of the Holy Sepulcher. Israel's financial hub is Tel Aviv.

The context of the calling of Abram—in which God instructed him to leave his country and his people and go to a new land—is completely different from the case of refugees in modern times. But the application may easily connect. Considering that, from the era when the pilgrims moved to this country on November 11, 1620, after a voyage of sixty-six days up to our modern era, millions of people who have moved to the United States of America were forced migrants. In other words, they were primarily people who were forced to leave their countries and habitual residence due to religious or political persecution.

The US Department of State's 2021 report reveals that, under the Immigration and Nationality Act (INA), a refugee is an alien who, generally, has experienced past persecution or has a well-founded fear of persecution on account of race, religion, nationality, membership in a particular social group, or political opinion. Individuals who meet this definition may be considered for either refugee status under Section 207 of the INA if they are outside the United States, or asylum status under Section 208 of the INA if they are already in the United States. Since the passage of the Refugee Act in 1980, which incorporated this definition of refugee into the INA, the United States has admitted more than 3.1 million refugees. The table 2 below shows the US refugee admission and asylum grants since 1980.

Refugee Admissions and Asylum Grants Since 1980

Fiscal Year	Refugee Arrivals	Individual Asylum Grants[d]	Annual Totals
1980	207,116	1,104	208,220
1981	159,252	1,175	160,427
1982	98,096	3,909	102,005
1983	61,218	7,215	68,433
1984	70,393	8,278	78,671
1985	67,704	4,585	72,289
1986	62,146	3,359	65,505
1987	64,528	4,062	68,590
1988	76,483	5,531	82,014
1989	107,070	6,942	114,012
1990	122,066	8,472	130,538
1991	113,389	5,035	118,424
1992	132,531	6,307	138,838
1993	119,448	9,543	128,991
1994	112,981	13,828	126,809
1995	99,974	20,703	120,677
1996	76,403	23,532	99,935
1997	70,488	22,939	93,427
1998	77,080	20,507	97,587
1999	85,525	26,571	112,096
2000	73,147	32,514	105,661
2001	69,304	39,148	108,452
2002	27,110	36,937	64,047
2003	28,422	28,743	57,165
2004	52,868	27,376	80,244
2005	53,813	25,304	79,117
2006	41,279	26,352	67,631
2007	48,281	25,318	73,599
2008	60,192	23,022	83,214
2009	74,654	22,303	96,957
2010	73,311	19,771	93,082
2011	56,424	23,569	79,993
2012	58,238	27,948	86,186
2013	69,925	24,996	94,921
2014	69,987	23,369	93,356
2015	69,933	26,011	95,944
2016	84,994	20,340	105,334
2017	53,716	26,568	80,284
2018	22,491	38,687	61,178
2019	30,000	46,203	76,203
Totals	3,101,980	768,076	3,870,056

Despite most of these people being forced into migration, God's hands were on it, as most of them, especially hardworking refugees who have moved to the United States, have found peace, security, and stability— "milk and honey"—in this country. Most refugees have achieved self-sufficiency and self-reliance and are making outstanding contributions to the national development of this land through labor, payment of taxes, employment creation, entrepreneurship, and religious and political participation. Also, many of them are assisting their extended family members and participating in community development efforts in their countries of origin. In other words, God's plan for sending refugees to the United States is not to harm anyone but, rather to make America a great and multicultural country. The US Refugee Admission Program has created opportunities for building a better future and can contribute to prosperity for all the people who live in this land because, as refugees and local Americans alike flourish as a result of welcoming refugees and immigrants in this country.

The book of Hebrews 13:2 reveals the importance of showing hospitality to strangers. "By this way many have shown hospitality to angels without knowing." I believe showing hospitality to strangers is one of the reasons America is blessed. Also, it justifies why the United States is the promised land for refugees.

In addition, when Italian explorer Christopher Columbus discovered America in 1492, he found the Native Americans, are also known as the American Indians. According to Worldometer 2021 statistics, the current population of the United States of America is 332,240,917 (as of Saturday, February 20, 2021). Most of these people's ancestors or parents came to the United States as refugees or immigrants. They moved to the United States in search of freedom, peace and security, and economic opportunities. This is the true evidence demonstrating that this country is the promised land for both immigrants and refugees. Immigrants and refugees have contributed to making America great and a prosperous country.

The US Refugee Admissions Program (USRAP)

According to the US Department of State's 2021 report, individuals outside the United States seeking admission as refugees under Section 207 of the INA are processed through the US Refugee Admissions Program (USRAP), which is managed by the Department of State in cooperation with the Department of Homeland Security (DHS) and Department of Health and Human Services (HHS). Those admitted as refugees are eligible for US government-funded resettlement assistance.

US Refugee Admissions Program: Overseas application and case processing

The first step for most people seeking refugee status is to register with the UNHCR the country to which they have fled. UNHCR determines if an individual qualifies as a refugee and, if so, works toward the best possible durable solution—safe return to the home country, local integration, or permanent resettlement in a third country. According to the UNCHR (2011):

> Resettlement involves the selection and transfer of refugees from a State in which they have sought protection to a third State which has agreed to admit them—as refugees—with permanent residence status. The status provided ensures protection against deportation and provides a resettled refugee and his/her family or dependents with access to rights similar to those enjoyed by nationals. Resettlement also carries with it the opportunity to eventually become a naturalized citizen of the resettlement country. The Office of the United Nations High Commissioner for Refugees (UNHCR) was established on January 1, 1951, by UN General Assembly Resolution 319 (IV). Resettlement serves three equally important functions. First, it is a tool to provide international protection and meet the specific needs of individual refugees whose life, liberty, safety, health, or other fundamental rights are at risk in the country where they have sought refuge. Second, it is a durable solution for larger numbers or groups of refugees, alongside the other durable solutions of voluntary repatriation and local integration. Third, it can be a tangible expression of international solidarity and a responsibility sharing mechanism, allowing States to help share responsibility

for refugee protection, and reduce problems impacting the country of asylum.

For instance, In Zimbabwe right now, refugees are experiencing serious food crises, as many of them have been reduced to one meal every two days. The country is seriously challenged by its own economic problems that have reduced most of its population to one meal a day. Refugees have no right to citizenship. Education outside Tongogara Camp is not free, and most refugees cannot afford. As a result, many refugee children and Zimbabwe citizens are unable to attend school because their parents, who are unemployed, cannot afford to pay school fees. Currently, there is only one primary and one secondary school in Tongogara Refugee Camp. The schools are overcrowded and beyond their capacity. As a result, most students are learning under trees and other open spaces without any shelter. This situation is robbing the refugee children and youth—who need education to prepare for their own future but are denied the opportunity due to macroeconomic challenges experienced in the country and UNHCR budgetary constraints—of possibility.

Refugee youth in Zimbabwe need work to help themselves. But they cannot find jobs because already over 80 percent of the qualified Zimbabwean workforce is unemployed. Refugees, especially those from the Democratic Republic of the Congo hosted in Zimbabwe and other African countries don't feel safe to return to their country because of continued insecurity, and Zimbabwean law does not provide for citizenship for refugees. The only sustainable solution for Congolese refugees living in refugee camps in Zimbabwe and other African countries, such as Kenya, Tanzania, Namibia, and Uganda, is humanitarian support and resettlement to a third country, such as the United States of America, Australia, Canada, Sweden, Norway, Denmark, and other developed countries that have the economic capacity and political will to receive vulnerable refugees through refugee resettlement programs.

Every year, the US president sends a report to Congress on the proposed number of refugees to be admitted in the next fiscal year, along with other information. When a US embassy or a specially trained nongovernmental organization refers a refugee applicant to the United States for resettlement, the case is first received and processed by a resettlement support center (RSC). The Department of State currently funds and manages seven RSCs around the world, operated by nongovernmental organizations (NGOs), international organizations, or US embassy contractors. Certain refugee applicants can start the application process with the RSC without a referral. This includes close relatives of asylum seekers and refugees already in the United States and applicants who belong to specific groups identified in statute or by the Department of State as eligible for direct access to the program.

Adjudication

According to the US Department of state's 2020 report, RSCs collect biographic and other information from the applicants to prepare cases for security screening, interview, and adjudication by US Citizenship and Immigration Services (USCIS). The secretary of Homeland Security has delegated to USCIS the authority to determine eligibility for refugee status under the INA. Refugee determinations under the INA are entirely discretionary. USCIS officers review the information that the RSC has collected and the results of security screening processes and conduct an in-person interview with each refugee applicant before deciding whether to approve him or her for classification as a refugee.

Post-adjudication processing

According to the US Department of State's 2020, report, if an applicant is conditionally approved for resettlement by USCIS, the RSC staff guide the refugee applicant through post-adjudication steps, including a health screening to identify medical needs and to ensure that those with a contagious disease do not enter the United States. The RSC also obtains a "sponsorship assurance" from a US-based resettlement agency that receives funding from PRM for reception and placement (R&P) assistance. Once all required steps are completed, the RSC refers the case to the International Organization for Migration (IOM) for transportation to the United States.

Transportation

According to the Department of Homeland Security and Department of Health and Human Services' 2020 report, the Department of State funds the international transportation of refugees resettled in the United States through a program administered by International Organization for Migration (IOM). The cost of transportation is provided to refugees in the form of a no-interest loan. Refugees are responsible for repaying these loans over time through their R&P providers, beginning six months after their arrival.

Cultural Orientation

According to the Department of Homeland Security and Department of Health and Human Services' 2020 report, the Department of State strives to ensure that refugees admitted to the United States are prepared for the changes they will experience by providing cultural orientation programs prior to departure. Every refugee family is offered a copy of "Welcome to the United States," a book developed with contributions from refugee resettlement workers, resettled refugees, and government officials that provides accurate information about initial resettlement. In addition, the Department of State funds one- to five-day predeparture orientation classes for eligible refugees at sites throughout the world. Refugees may also access cultural orientation information through the US State Department website that is translated into seven languages and provides information in numerous modes to meet all literacy levels, as well as a new mobile application.

Reception and placement (R&P)

According to the US Department of States' 2020 report unlike asylees, who arrive in the United States on their own, refugees selected for resettlement through U.S. Refugee Admissions Program are eligible for R&P assistance. Each refugee approved for admission to the United States is sponsored by a nonprofit resettlement agency participating in the R&P program under a cooperative agreement with the Department of State. The sponsoring resettlement agency is responsible for placing refugees with one of its local affiliates and for providing initial services.

The Department of State's standard cooperative agreement with each of the resettlement agencies specifies the services the agency must provide. The R&P program provides resettlement agencies a one-time payment per refugee to assist with expenses during a refugee's first three months in the United States, but the program anticipates that sponsoring agencies will contribute significant cash or in-kind resources to supplement US government funding.

I and my family members were received by World Relief. This agency did a tremendous job. Professional staff members provided us with all the support needed during the first three months after our arrival. After three months, World Relief continued to provide guidance together with other organizations, churches, and individuals. They encouraged me to start a 501(c)(3) nonprofit organization, Refugee Empowerment Network, which is now complementing their efforts. REN exists to show a generous welcome to refugees and empower them so they can integrate successfully and sustainably into their local communities. We are a registered nonprofit organization dedicated to providing practical, life-changing resources. We are champions for refugee vitality and resourcefulness in refugee camps and resettlement cities. We seek to build bridges and develop a multicultural connection between refugees, American churches, and American people.

Our vision is that refugees and vulnerable groups are empowered, independent community members. Our services include but aren't limited to:

- *Needs assessment.* We assess the needs of refugees and vulnerable groups on a case-by-case basis, both in the United States and abroad.
- *English as a second language (ESL).* We provide English lessons from beginner to advanced levels to refugees in the United States and assist them in integrating into the US society.
- *Basic training.* We also provide basic training on understanding the American culture, systems, and laws. This includes education on the American Constitution and learning and practice of civic questions and answers to prepare refugees to take and pass the naturalization test. Other training programs and activities are focused on human rights education, conflict prevention, and fighting gender-based violence. We seek to promote peaceful conflict resolution and conflict transformation in the global south, trauma awareness raising and healing among refugees, enable leadership development and transformation, support beneficial family dynamics, and contribute to reducing domestic violence in the global south.
- *Relief.* We provide household items such as food, clothing, and furniture; rental assistance; school supplies; and other necessities to help new arrival refugees and vulnerable groups meet their immediate needs.
- *Employment and training assistance.* We provide job-oriented training workshops, seminars, case management, mentorship, and coaching

services to refugees and vulnerable groups. We encourage them to be productive at work and demonstrate good working behavior and practices. We also network with employers and community leaders to hire refugees at their workplaces and help them to become self-sufficient and independent community members.

- *Entrepreneurship and financial literacy.* We provide basic training on entrepreneurship and good financial management practices, including budgeting and financial planning.
- *Education and professional development.* We provide orientation services for refugee access to lifelong education and training, including college and university studies. We seek to provide sponsorships to refugees and vulnerable groups to attend practical short-term professional training such as information communication and technology, truck driving, secretarial courses, housekeeping, senior care, baby and child care certification, food and beverages management, hotel and restaurant management, hospitality, and auto mechanics.
- *Microfinance.* We seek to create microfinance funds to promote entrepreneurship among refugees and vulnerable groups in the global south and enable them to venture into income-generating activities, create employment opportunities, and attain household food and income security.
- *Refugee housing.* We seek to educate refugees and create for them opportunities for quality affordable housing and help them become self-sufficient and transcend their difficult situations. REN seeks to partner with other agencies, private businesses, and institutions in developing affordable housing and provides counseling, education, and advocacy for the benefit of low and moderate-income refugee households.

REN also seek to provide services that promote responsible parenting, responsible citizenship, youth engagement, and mentoring.

Refugee Empowerment Network is grateful to many churches and organizations for assistance and support, among them Bethesda Community Church, Southcliff Baptist Church, and Kennedale Baptist Church. We are grateful to our individual donors, who have donated to support the implementation of our programs and services. We are also grateful for our partnerships with Fatherhood Coalition of Tarrant County, Hope Literacy, Fort Worth Hope Center, New Mount Rose Missionary Baptist Church, Cornerstone Assistance Network, Texas Christian University, and Cooperative Baptist Fellowship Refugee Ministries.

REN's 2021 to 2023 goals include but are not limited to:

1. Contribute to strengthening integration and inclusion of refugees in American community.
2. Increase our fundraising through individual donors, church donations, grants, and corporate partners.
3. Enhance training, education, and employment program and services for refugees.
4. Build partnerships and network with others to empower refugees by helping them to help themselves.
5. Provide relief such as food and household items to meet immediate felt needs of vulnerable refugees and partner with other community service providers.

Where are refugees resettled?

According to the US Department of States (2021), representatives from the resettlement agencies meet frequently to review the biographic information and other case records sent by the Department of State's overseas resettlement support centers (RSC), seeking to match the needs of each incoming refugee with the specific resources available in US communities. Through this process, they determine which resettlement agency will sponsor each refugee and where he or she will be initially resettled in the United States. Many refugees have family or close friends already in the United States, and resettlement agencies make every effort to reunite them. Others are placed where they have the best opportunity for success through employment, with the assistance of strong community services. Agencies place refugees through a network of approximately two hundred local affiliates operating in communities throughout the United States. Through its local affiliates, each agency monitors the resources that each community offers (for example, availability of affordable and safe housing, school capacity, medical care, and employment opportunities).

What happens when refugees arrive?

According to the US Department of States' 2021 report, upon arrival in the United States, all refugees are met by someone from the local resettlement affiliate or a family member or friend. They are taken to their initial housing, which is equipped with essential furnishings, appropriate food, and other necessities. The resettlement agencies assist refugees during their initial resettlement in the United States, including helping them enroll in employment services, register youth for school, apply for social security cards, and connect with necessary social or language services.

In coordination with officially supported refugee service and assistance programs, resettlement agencies focus on assisting refugees to achieve economic self-sufficiency through employment as soon as possible after their arrival in the United States. Refugees receive employment authorization upon arrival and are encouraged to become employed as soon as possible. The R&P program is limited to the first three months after arrival, but the Department of Health and Human Services' Office of Refugee Resettlement works through the states and other nongovernmental organizations to provide longer-term cash and medical assistance, as well as language, employment, and social services.

Table 4. Estimated Cost for Refugee Processing and Resettlement

Agency	FY 2020 Availability (in millions)	FY 2021 Estimated Availability (in millions)
DHS/USCIS USRAP processing[13]	$38	$41
Department of State/PRM USRAP admissions[14]	$333	$343
HHS/ORR benefits and services[15]	$561	$430
Totals	**$932**	**$814**

Source: US Department of State (2021)

However, many resettlement agencies, both locally and overseas, are currently operating below their capacity due to funding challenges. There is a need to increase funding support to enable refugee resettlement agencies and other organizations providing direct services to refugees to effectively provide their services to refugees.

Effects of the COVID-19 Pandemic

According to a 2021 US government Proposed Refugee Admission for Fiscal Year report to Congress, refugee resettlement in the United States decreased significantly in fiscal year 2020 due to the COVID-19 pandemic. Due to travel restrictions in and out of refugee processing sites worldwide, USRAP suspended refugee arrivals from March 19 to July 29, 2020, except for emergency cases. USRAP resumed general refugee arrivals July 30, 2020, with additional health measures specified by the Centers for Disease Control and Prevention (CDC). However, reduced flight availability due to the general decrease in demand for international travel meant a slow pace of refugee resettlement in the United States through the rest of fiscal year 2020. Almost seven thousands of the eighteen thousand refugee slots available under the fiscal year 2020 Presidential Determination went unused. The president's proposed refugee admissions ceiling for fiscal year 2021 incorporates these places that might have been used if not for the COVID-19 pandemic.

Permanent Residence and Citizenship through Naturalization

The US Citizenship and Immigration Services (USCI) is the government agency responsible for providing green cards to refugees. The process of obtaining the green card for resettled refugees takes about two years, and citizenship is obtainable after five years on condition that the refugee can pass a basic civics and English language test.

Refugee Empowerment Network provides English as a second language training to non-English speaking refugees and prepares them for the naturalization test. REN provides guidance to refugees on how to fill out their N-400 forms and submit their application for naturalization.

Conclusion

This chapter focused on the importance of the United States of America's Refugee Resettlement Program. It explained the process of resettling refugees into the United States—examining the selection process, health and security screening, travel and arrival of refugees, and the granting of permanent residence and citizenship through naturalization. The United States Refugee Resettlement Program provides great practical possibilities for refugees to meet their human needs. It enables them to participate in national economic development and politics in the United States through labor, entrepreneurship, employment creation, and payment of taxes. And it allows them, by becoming active citizens, to be a blessing to others within and outside the United States' borders.

This chapter has revealed why the United States of America is the promised land for people who've experienced religious persecution or been forced to leave their home countries due to war, conflict, and political instability. The US Refugee Resettlement Program is an answer to the prayers of those concerned with the plight of refugees. It provides tangible results and opportunities for the social and economic inclusion of refugees. Many refugees are achieving their American dream of self-sufficiency and self-reliance and are also managing to help other people within and outside the United States. These opportunities were not available to refugees when they were living in refugee camps in Africa before relocating to the United States.

The following chapter gives stories of change that reveal the outcome and impact of the US Refugee Resettlement Program.

CHAPTER 7

TESTIMONIES ON THE OUTCOME AND IMPACT OF THE US REFUGEE SETTLEMENT PROGRAM

Introduction

This chapter focuses on the testimonies and stories of significant change provided by individual Congolese refugees who were resettled to the state of Texas in the United States through the US Refugee Resettlement Program. It explains how a range of human needs such as distributive justice, safety and security, belonging and love, self-esteem, personal fulfillment, cultural security, freedom, and participation are being met here in the United States. Most of these needs—such as self-esteem, personal fulfillment, cultural security, freedom, and participation—were not easy to meet when refugees were still living in refugee camps in Africa.

This chapter also provides a few testimonies given by institutions and organizations that provide different types of services to refugees. The story of change will reveal the outcomes and impact of these crucial humanitarian programs and the need for continued support and collective efforts in addressing the plight of refugees around the world. Here, too, we'll look at the need for collaboration between various partners, in particular resettlement states, international organizations, and nongovernmental organizations (NGOs). Government policies must be enabled, and financial support and assistance to organizations involved in providing services, such as resettlement, training, education, and employment programs that build the capacity of refugees in the United States of America and around the world must be increased. This will help resettled refugees, especially youth, to help themselves and become active and independent community members.

Impact of refugee resettlement around the world

According to the UNHCR 2021 report:

> Over the past sixty years resettlement has provided millions of people with protection and the opportunity to build new lives for themselves and their families. The refugees have made important contributions to the countries that received them and active engagement with resettled refugees has also fostered awareness and support for refugees among the publics of resettlement countries. Resettlement has also brought about positive results that go well beyond those that are usually viewed as a resettlement outcome. In the face of a continued influx of refugees, the use of resettlement has convinced countries of first asylum to keep open their borders, thereby avoiding massive loss of life. In other situations, resettlement has played a key role in unlocking the impasses in protracted refugee situations and opening the possibilities of other durable solutions. Offering resettlement places to refugees in need is also an active expression of responsibility sharing with the countries that host the bulk of the world's refugees. Overall, resettlement is a dynamic and flexible tool, and when done effectively and with strategic vision, the results of resettlement can be powerful beyond the direct impact on the persons resettled.

The following sections reveal practical outcomes and the impact of the US Refugee Resettlement Program based on testimonies given by resettled Congolese refugees.

Distributive justice

Distributive justice is the need for the fair allocation of resources among all members. It focuses on adopting positive measures to ensure that all policies, whether economic, social, cultural, or legal, benefit all members equally. In the United States, refugees and their children are viewed as equal members of society with needs to be met. Unlike in refugee camps, refugee children attend free, quality elementary and high schools in this country. Many refugee children and youths are doing very well with their studies. A few of them have already moved on to universities and colleges. The US government has provided scholarships, grants, and financial aid to deserving refugee youth. For example, my two sons, Obed and Kijana, were accepted in a local university and will begin their academic studies in August. One of them is interested in mechanical engineering, and the other will study political science and international relations. Access to lifelong, quality education is a cornerstone to refugee empowerment, self-esteem, self-sufficiency, and self-reliance.

Refugees, including the elderly and the sick, have access to medical aid, social security assistance, and food stamps. These kinds of services and resources are not available to refugees in the camps.

One of the Congolese ladies said:

> Before relocating to the US, I lived in Nyarugusu Refugee Camp in Tanzania for eighteen years. Life in the camp was not easy, and I was always sick. Every month, I was spending seven to twenty days in a hospital bed, and my situation was deteriorating. However, when I moved to the US in 2016, up to date, I have never spent a night in a hospital bed. I receive medical supplied every month, and my health condition has greatly improved. This makes me believe that God has used the Refugee Resettlement Program to add more days to my life. Sometimes people die before their time due to poor living conditions and lack of quality medical services. There is a great difference between the living conditions in the refugee camp and my new life here in the US. I thank the Lord for bringing me

here. My coming here is an answered prayer and God's favor upon my life and the lives of many other refugees. (2021 interview response)

Another lady told her story as well:

Before relocating to the US, I lived in the city of Lusaka, Republic of Zambia, as an urban refugee. My husband and I managed to buy a piece of land in Lusaka, and we built a house. We also built some rooms that were used by tenants. We generated our monthly income by venturing into small businesses and by collecting monthly rentals from our tenants. When my husband died in 2009, things became so hard for me and my family. We were resettled to the US in August 2014. Although, I am no longer working because of my advanced age, I thank the Lord and the US government for bringing us here. My children are working, and they hope to build a better future for themselves and their children in this country. My major challenge is the language barrier; I am not yet able to fluently speak the English language, but I need to get US citizenship. I am willing to learn the English language. I thank the US government for the Medicaid, social security assistance, and food stamps provided. (2021 interview)

The above testimonies are clear evidence of distributive justice through the fair allocation of resources among all members of society, including refugees who have resettled in this country through the US Refugee Resettlement Program.

Self-esteem

Many refugees have lost their self-esteem due to a dependence syndrome instituted in refugee camps. In most camps, refugees are not allowed to work. As a result, they are totally dependent on humanitarian aid provided to them through the UNHCR. Refugees' esteem needs—in terms of achievement, status, responsibility, and reputation—are being restored through the resettlement program.

All human beings, including refugees, have big dreams and desire to achieve great things in their personal, family, and community lives. This can only be achieved within the context of favorable policies, a stable economic environment, and fair practices. The United States has provided this enabling environment for refugees, and many are now working and taking care of their own needs without depending on aid. For example, take this account of a male refugee:

> When we were living in the refugee camp, I was totally broke and could not afford to buy anything for my wife and children because I was not working. With the hard life in the camp, I used to look down upon myself. Every time my children or my wife asked me to buy them something, I was viewing it as provocation. I was unable to help them and lived in anger, which resulted in conflict in our home. I was always feeling insecure and irresponsible because I was failing to take care of my family's needs. Life in the camp could not enable me to buy a bike that cost only between $50 and $100. I was living in deep poverty because of unemployment. However, when I relocated to the US through the Refugee Resettlement Program, I have managed to find a job that has enabled me to take care of my family's basic needs. I pay rent on a monthly basis; I buy and eat the food I need. I take my family to eat at restaurants on a regular basis. I now own two vehicles, which I never dreamed to own when I was living in the camp. I now live at peace with my family members because my anger is gone. I can conclude that the Refugee Resettlement Program restored my self-esteem. (2021 interview response)

Testimony shared by Karen Morrow

Karen is the Director for Refugee Ministries at the Cooperative Baptist Fellowship. She works hand in hand with Refugee Empowerment Network through partnership. Karen has served among refugee and asylee populations for the past twenty-four years, first in Europe working among Kurdish asylum seekers for twelve years and, for the last twelve, years working among refugees resettled through the refugee resettlement program in Fort Worth, Texas. She said:

> I walk alongside refugee families as they acclimate to life here in the US, being their cultural guide and friend. I help them learn how to access systems that help them become more self-sufficient and live life successfully. I also help in providing items for household setup, clothing, food, new babies, and special occasions—Christmas, Easter, and back to school. I have taught basic ESL and citizenship as well as specialized trainings relevant to life here in the US. I have helped develop the Ready for School program—a twenty-week family literacy program for limited English-speaking preschoolers and their parents. We teach basic literacy, math, motor, and social skills needed to enter pre-K. I have also helped to establish Hope Library for refugee children in a church across the street from an apartment complex where many refugee families live.
>
> Another emphasis is educating Americans on the refugee experience, resettlement process, and how they can be become involved in welcoming refugees and immigrants.
>
> Some of the refugees that I have walked alongside of now have university and graduate degrees, are now working professional jobs, as well as others who are now homeowners. Other refugees have learned English, and many have become US citizens. These accomplishments were from their hard work. My ministry was in helping to teach them, helping them find necessary resources and opportunities. I encourage them along the way as a mentor and friend.
>
> The refugee preschoolers in our Ready for School program have transitioned well into school. The greatest joy is being

a welcomed member of their families. From missions' perspective, I believe God is working among the nations and is bringing the nations to our doorstep, where they have access to Christian witness in word and deed. Scripturally, I believe we are called to welcome the foreigner living among us and to serve the widows and orphans. Many refugees come with strong Christian faith and they themselves are a part of God's redemptive work in the world. Those refugees from other faiths who come to know Christ here are key in taking the good news of Christ back to their home country.

All people have been created in the image of God with gifts and talents. Refugees bring those gifts and talents with them and can use them for the good of all. I believe each culture has its strengths and beauty, which add to US culture. It has been a blessing to see refugees work hard, be able to purchase a home, and see their children succeed in school and university. Refugees themselves begin serving in their community and taking leadership roles in the workplace.

However, language has been a challenge with many of the refugee groups coming. Limited to no English makes it difficult to help refugees initially. The need to work to support their families leaves them with limited opportunity for language learning, which in turn limits their economic opportunities and opportunity to live successfully. Some refugees come very educated from their home countries, while others are illiterate in their mother tongue. Lack of previous education coupled with trauma makes transition to life and learning here much more difficult and serving these refugees incredibly challenging.

The testimony shared by Karen reveals the outcomes and impact of the US Refugee Resettlement Program. Also, it reveals how a language barrier and a low level of education limits many refugees from achieving self-esteem and self-sufficiency. Refugee Empowerment Network and its partners would like to continue providing training and education services to empower refugees. However, we will not be able to achieve much without your financial support. Therefore, we are prayerfully and kindly asking you to help us help them.

Personal fulfillment

Personal fulfillment is the need to reach one's potential in all areas of life. For example, one refugee who serves as the leader for the Congolese refugee community in Fort Worth Texas said, "When I was in the refugee camp, I always dreamed to have my own property in an urban area. When I relocated to the US, I worked hard with my wife and children, and we have managed to move from renting to the ownership of a six-bedroom house in Arlington. We are managing to pay mortgage. Although I have not yet finished paying my mortgage, I feel proud because my dream has been fulfilled. The fulfillment of my dream was made possible through the US government Refugee Resettlement Program" (2021 interview response).

Another couple said:

> When we were in the refugee camp in Namibia, we were confined to depend on the UNHCR assistance only. Although, we tried to engage in small income-generating activities through our own initiative, the conditions were limiting us from fulfilling our dreams. We are pleased to the say that four years after our relocation to the United States through Refugee Resettlement Program, we managed to move from renting to home ownership and we are paying the mortgage on monthly basis because we are both employed. We joyfully and proudly bring our monthly incomes to our home and family. We bought a new five-bedroom [house] in a better location in San Antonio, Texas. Unlike in the refugee camp, we can take care of our own needs and make the right choices and plans for our personal lives and that of our children. Also, we are sponsoring students and send remittance to help our extended family members in Africa

on a regular basis. These possibilities have given us a sense of personal fulfillment. (2021 interview response)

On the other hand, it's important to mention that many refugees who were resettled in this country still experience financial challenges when it comes to meeting their basic expenses. This is because their wages are low and cannot sustain them. As a result, many work beyond their normal working hours to try to increase their incomes. Most of them work ten hours a day six to seven days every week. Others work two to three jobs, which makes them sick because human beings cannot work like a machine.

In addition, working three jobs or long hours every week makes many parents irresponsible and irrelevant, as they no longer have time to spend together with their children. And many couples are in danger because they can no longer satisfy each other sexually. They are always tired because they come home already exhausted. But constant sex between a married couple can strengthen the marriage union and reduce stress. Most importantly, it may protect both the husband and wife from falling into the sin of engaging in extramarital sexual relationships or sexual immorality. This sin violates the principle of biblical marriage stated in Matthew 19:4–5 and in 1 Corinthians 6:19–20. The Bible encourages us to flee from it (1 Corinthians 6:18).

I've also observed that many refugees have no time to keep their homes and kitchens clean. When they come from work, they just sleep, and when they wake up, they are ready to go back to work. As such, homes and kitchens are left dirty. This situation should not be allowed to continue because hygiene and cleanliness are important for human health.

There is a need to assist this group of refugees. Helping them learn English is a vital step. So is providing professional training that will upgrade their skills. Forklift operation certification, professional truck driving instruction, GED preparation, and other job-oriented short courses can enable them to find better paying jobs and have time to rest and to spend with their families at home. Without that, they will not be able to fulfill their American dreams; most couples will be likely to divorce, and children will be taken away by Child Protective Services (CPS).

However, it does not help anyone to gain a lot of money but lose his or her spouse and children. Nothing in the world is more important than one's own family. Besides God, our next highest priorities are our spouses and children.

Other refugees are frustrated because they work in jobs that do not match their skills and credentials. For example, a qualified medical doctor, nurse, or lawyer, may find him or herself serving as cashiers, meat packers, cleaners, and grocery store clerks or employed at warehouses, market stores, hospitals, and airports. They feel humiliated, disappointed, and unable to fulfill their personal goals. There is a need to assess these refugees' qualifications through equivalence certifications and offer them professional jobs and salaries that match their level of education and professional experiences. This will help them to achieve their personal goals or American dreams.

Personal fulfillment goes hand in hand with identity, which goes beyond a psychological "sense of self." Identity is a sense of self in relation to the outside world. It becomes a problem when one's identity is not recognized as legitimate or when it is considered inferior or is threatened by others with different identifications.

The US government provides refugees with identity documents that give them legitimate recognition as equal to other US residents. Resettled refugees are allowed to work and can create their own jobs, just like any other ordinary American citizen. In addition, refugees are allowed to apply for American citizenship through naturalization.

Cultural security

Cultural security is related to identity and the need for recognition of one's language, traditions, religion, cultural values, ideas, and concepts.

I am currently pastoring a Swahili congregation at Bethesda Community Church (BCC). BCC is a multicultural and multigenerational Bible-believing church located in Haltom City, Texas. The church is unique, and it comprises six different language services that meet for worship every Sunday in different rooms. Services are conducted in English, Burmese, French, Kirundi-Kinyarwanda, Spanish, and Swahili.

Our senior pastor, J. Daniel Smith, and his entire leadership team gave us a green light and are providing support for each group to conduct their services in their own language, Christian traditions, and values. This provides cultural security to refugees and immigrants. Most members of our African language services feel at home away from home.

The greatest joy is that, while we conduct our services in different rooms and different languages, we all serve one God in Jesus Christ's name. This makes this church unique, fast-growing, unstoppable, and relevant. The Bible says, "After this I looked, and there before me was a great multitude that no one could count, from every nation, tribe, people and language, standing before the throne and before the Lamb. They were wearing white robes and were holding palm branches in their hands. And they cried out in a loud voice: 'Salvation belongs to our God, who sits on the throne, and to the Lamb.' All the angels were standing around the throne and around the elders and the four living creatures. They fell down on their faces before the throne and worshiped God" (Revelation 7:9–11). This is a beautiful picture of how believers from every nation, tribe, and language will stand before our God and His Son Jesus Christ in days to come.

The promotion of a multicultural and multigenerational church is particularly important because it is in line with the Great Commission of our Lord and Savior Jesus Christ as stated in Matthew 28:19–20.

Recently, we conducted a membership class for the Swahili service congregants. The training provides the opportunity for them to become effective members of the Bethesda Community Church.

Freedom

Freedom is the condition of having no physical, political, or civil restraints and having the capacity to exercise choice in all aspects of one's life.

Unlike refugee camps in Zimbabwe and other African countries, where refugee encampment policies confine refugees, restricting their freedom of movement, US laws and policies provide conditions that give refugees freedom of movement. They are able to travel anywhere within and outside of the United States. In addition, refugees are allowed to live in any place they choose throughout the United States.

Participation

Participation is the need to be able to actively partake in and influence civil society.

Unlike in refugee camps, refugees in the United States can participate in political and civil activities, especially after obtaining US citizenship. They can vote or be elected to take up public offices at different levels and capacities.

The US Constitution states, "No Person except a natural born Citizen, or a Citizen of the United States, at the time of the Adoption of this Constitution, shall be eligible to the Office of President; neither shall any Person be eligible to hold the Office who shall not have attained to the Age of thirty-five Years, and been fourteen Years a Resident within the United States."

This provision gives naturalized refugees the ability to serve at various positions in the US government, except the office of president:

> "The US Bill of Rights, provides for the freedom of religion, speech, the press, or the right of the people to assemble peaceably, and to petition the government for a redress of grievances. It also provides for the right of the people to keep and bear arms … In all criminal prosecutions, the accused shall enjoy the right to a speedy and public trial, by an impartial jury of the State and district wherein the crime shall have been committed; which district shall have been previously ascertained by law, and to be informed of the nature and cause of the accusation; to be confronted with the witnesses against him; to have compulsory process for obtaining witnesses in his favor; and to have the assistance of counsel for his defense"(US Bill of Rights, US Constitution, 1791).

In addition, one of the greatest things that makes this country unique is that none is above the law. And the United States upholds respect for human life. Lack of respect for human life and a state of lawlessness were among the major causes that forced many people to leave their countries of origin and habitual residence and seek asylum in other countries before relocating to the United States. Most refugees admire the peace, security, political systems, and economic stability in the United States. The prayer and hope is that refugees can be resourced and equipped to continue participating in the economic, social, and political development of this country and also contribute to the reconstruction of their countries of origin in the future.

Based on the above-named comparative evidence, I am lobbying the US government, the American people, and US churches to support President Joseph Biden's executive order to increase the ceiling and speed up the process of welcoming new refugees to the United States through the US Refugee Resettlement Program.

Conclusion

This chapter focused on the testimonies and stories of significant change provided by individual Congolese refugees who were resettled to the State of Texas in the United States through the US Refugee Resettlement Program. It explained how refugees here in the United States are able to meet a range of human needs. Most of these needs—among the self-esteem, personal fulfillment, cultural security, freedom, and participation—were not easy to meet when refugees were still living in refugee camps in Africa. Therefore, there is a need to continue assisting refugees through the Refugee Resettlement Program and by providing other services, such as training, education, and employment solutions that will help refugees meet their human needs and achieve self-sufficiency and self-reliance.

The following chapter discusses the need to contribute to the promotion of sustainable peace and security in countries affected by war to allow most refugees who could not be resettled to a third country to return to their countries of origin and habitual residence. Most importantly, we must trust God in prayer and action.

CHAPTER 8

THE CRY FOR PEACE WITHOUT RECOURSE TO WAR

Introduction

This last chapter focuses on the cry for peace through mediation. Peace is the absence of war. Many countries in Africa—among them, the United Republic of Tanzania, Botswana, and Zambia—have experienced decades of peace, stability, and peaceful political leadership transition. The United States is among the most stable countries politically and economically. As such, Americans enjoy the political gift of peace and security. Americans can plan proactively for their future and the future of their children and grandchildren.

However, other countries, such as the Democratic Republic of the Congo (DRC) have experienced decades of conflicts and wars. Countries affected by war have lost millions of innocent lives. From 1999 to date, the DRC has lost over 12 million lives. In war-torn countries, economic and social infrastructures are destroyed. Poverty, unemployment, suffering, poor health, shortage of food, and corruption increase. Women and girls are raped. War-torn countries are producers of large flows of refugees and internally displaced people. "Eight out of 10 of the world's poorest countries are suffering, or have recently suffered, from large scale violent conflict," (Stewart 2002). The question is, how can we promote sustainable peace in war-affected countries and the world at large without using militarily interventions?

Understanding the root causes of war

To effectively address the problems of war, there is need to understand its root causes, actors, and dynamics. Although causes for conflict are multifaceted, most experts in conflict mapping and resolution, agree that poverty; greediness, corruption, political intolerance, and injustice; low levels of education; political interference by world or external powers; illegal trade; and social and economic inequalities between groups are among the highest causes of conflicts that lead to war. To tackle such problems, there is need for multidimensional approaches; political willingness; and robust support at local, regional, and internal levels. The following sections will describe some approaches that were used in addressing the causes of conflicts and war in Africa and other parts of the world.

Boutros Boutros-Ghali: An Agenda for Peace

"On June 17, 1992, pursuant to the presidential statement adopted by the Security Council at its summit meeting on January 31, 1992, then UN Secretary General Boutros Boutros-Ghali submitted to the council a report entitled "An Agenda for Peace: Preventive Diplomacy, Peacemaking, and Peacekeeping." (UN,1992). The report contained, as requested, his analysis and recommendations on ways of strengthening and making more efficient, within the framework and provisions of the charter, the capacity of the United Nations for preventive diplomacy, peacemaking, and peacekeeping—to which he had added the closely related concept of peace building.

"An Agenda for Peace" aimed to identify, at the earliest possible stage, situations that could produce conflict and to try, through diplomacy, to remove the sources of danger before violence resulted. Where conflict had erupted, it aimed to engage in peacemaking aimed at resolving the issues that had led to conflict; through peacekeeping, to work to preserve peace where fighting had been halted; and to assist in implementing agreements achieved by the peacemakers. And it aimed to stand ready to assist in peace building in its differing contexts and to address the deepest causes of conflict—economic despair, social injustice, and political oppression. The Secretary-General stressed that this wider mission for the Organization would demand the concerted attention and effort of individual States

—which remained the foundation stone of this work —regional and non-governmental organizations, and the entire United Nations system.

The secretary-general provided the following definitions for the key terms used in his report:

a) preventive diplomacy was action taken to prevent disputes from arising between parties, to prevent existing disputes from escalating into conflicts and to limit the spread of the latter when they occurred.

b) peacemaking was action to bring hostile parties to agreement, essentially through such peaceful means as those foreseen in Chapter VI of the Charter of the United Nations;

c) peacekeeping was the deployment of a United Nations presence in the field, hitherto with the consent of all the parties concerned, normally involving United Nations military and/or police personnel and frequently civilians as well — it was a technique that expanded the possibilities for both the prevention of conflict and the making of peace;

d) post-conflict peacebuilding was action to identify and support structures which would tend to strengthen and solidify peace in order to avoid a relapse into conflict. These four areas of action, taken together and carried out with the backing of all Members, offered, he maintained, a coherent contribution towards securing peace in the spirit of the Charter.

Commencing with preventive diplomacy, the Secretary-General observed that it could be performed by the Secretary-General personally or through senior staff or specialized agencies or programmes, by the Security Council or by the General Assembly, as well as by regional organizations in cooperation with the United Nations. It required confidence-building measures; it needed early warning based on information-gathering and fact-finding; and it could involve preventive deployment and, in some situations, demilitarized zones. He stressed the need for an increased resort to fact-finding, in accordance with the Charter—initiated either by the Secretary-General, to enable him to meet his responsibilities under the Charter, including Article 99, or by the Security Council or the General Assembly. Various forms of fact-finding mission could be employed according to the requirements of the situation. A request by a State for the sending of a United Nations fact-finding mission to its territory should be considered without undue delay. In addition to collecting information on which a decision for further action could be taken, such a mission could in some instances help to defuse a dispute by its presence, indicating to the parties that the Organization, and in particular the Security Council, was actively seized of the matter as a present or potential threat to international security. The Secretary-General added that, in exceptional circumstances, the Council might itself meet away from Headquarters, in order not only to inform itself directly, but also to bring the authority of the Organization to bear on a given situation. In connection with early warning, he pointed to the need for close cooperation between the various specialized agencies and functional offices of the United Nations. He recommended, moreover, that the Security Council invite a reinvigorated and restructured Economic and Social Council to provide reports, in accordance with Article 65 of the Charter, on those economic and social developments that might, unless mitigated, threaten international peace and security. As for preventive deployment, the Secretary-General suggested that the time had come to consider such action in various circumstances, with the consent of the parties concerned: for example, in conditions of internal conflict; in an inter-State dispute; or where one nation feared a cross-border attack.

Turning to peacemaking, the Secretary-General noted that Chapter VI of the Charter set forth a comprehensive list of peaceful means for the resolution of conflict. He also called attention to the power of the Security Council, under Articles 36 and 37 of the Charter, to recommend to Member States the submission of a dispute to the International Court of Justice, arbitration, or other dispute-settlement mechanisms. He recommended that he be authorized, pursuant to Article 96 (2), to take advantage of the advisory competence of the Court and that other United Nations organs that already enjoyed such authorization turn to the Court more frequently for advisory opinions. He stressed that when peacemaking required the imposition of sanctions under Article 41, States confronted with special economic problems should not only have the right to consult the Security Council, as provided by Article 50, but should also have the "realistic possibility" of having their difficulties addressed. In that context, he recommended that the Council devise a set of measures involving the financial institutions and other components of the United Nations system that could be put in place to insulate States from such difficulties. On the use of military force, the Secretary General observed that it was the essence of the concept of collective security that, if peaceful means failed, the measures provided in Chapter VII should be used, on the decision of the Security Council, to maintain or restore international peace and security. Under Article 42 of the Charter, the Council itself had the authority to take military action for that purpose.

The agenda for peace was a great plan. And it's still achieving great results in terms of promoting international peace by encouraging all actors or parties involved in conflict and active violence to join hands and share in the responsibility of preventing conflict, protecting people, and to rebuilding peace. However, since cases of wars and violent conflicts are still increasing around the world, there is need for more debates, brainstorming, and theories and more practices that favor diplomacy through dialogue, negotiation, and mediation in addressing root causes of conflicts.

The next section focuses on multitrack diplomacy. I am emphasizing this because the US Refugee Resettlement Program can only solve part of refugees' problems. The best solution to the refugee problem writ large is peace. When there is sustainable peace and security in countries affected by war, refugees can peacefully return to their home countries through voluntary repatriation. This is the process in which refugees return in safety and with dignity to their country of origin or habitual residence and re-avail themselves of national protection.

Multitrack diplomacy

According to Julia et al. (2020), multitrack approaches to peace processes can be understood as a way of considering different peace-building initiatives taking place at different levels of society, with the intention of leveraging the positive impact of linkages between initiatives, while preventing or mitigating the negative impact. This model is built on three key elements, namely dialogue, negotiation, and mediation. Although multitrack diplomacy seems to be an expensive approach to conflict resolution and peace building, it is useful because it promotes the participation of various actors, such as top-level political or government leaders, experts in conflict resolution, business leaders, and private citizens or individuals at the grassroot levels. It involves research, education, and training institutions; peace activists such as civil society organizations; religious leaders and churches; funding organizations; media; and public opinion. If all these groups genuinely worked together without any negative external interference, the result would lead to conflict transformation and sustainable peace.

For example, Johan Galtung who is internationally recognized as "the father of the discipline of peace and conflict studies" (Transcend Media Service, 2020). Galtung believes that "peace can be achieved without recourse to war. He emphasized on mediation rather than war. Galtung theorized peacebuilding by calling for systems that would create sustainable peace. The peacebuilding structures required to address the root causes of conflict and support local capacity for peace management and conflict resolution. He believes that the culture of violence can be overcome through change of mindsets, and human behavior".

Galtung (1996) scholarly article gave the beautiful distinction between 'negative peace' and 'positive peace'. Negative peace refers to the absence of violence. When, for example, a ceasefire is enacted, a negative peace will ensue. It is negative because something undesirable stopped happening, the violence stopped, the oppression ended. But positive peace is filled with positive content such as restoration of relationships, the creation of social systems that serve the needs of the whole population and the constructive resolution of conflict. Peace does not mean the total absence of any conflict. It means the absence of violence in all forms and the unfolding of conflict in a constructive way. Peace therefore exists where people are interacting non-violently and are managing their conflict positively—with respectful attention to the legitimate needs and interest of all concerned. He concluded that peace can be achieved through cooperation for mutual and equal benefits.

Other scholars, such as Nelson Mandela, Gandhi, and Martin Luther King Jr. played significant roles in promoting peace without recourse to war. For example, Nelson Mandela served as the president of South Africa from 1994 to 1999. He left a legacy of forgiveness and racial reconciliation.

For instance, Mahatma Gandhi is viewed as one of the greatest preachers of peace the world has seen after Buddha and Christ. His notion of peace is focused on nonviolence, and forgiveness. He defined world peace as an ideal of freedom, peace, and happiness among and within all nations and/or people. It generally includes an idea of planetary non-violence by which nations willingly cooperate, either voluntarily or by virtue of a system of governance that prevents warfare. Gandhi said, "If we have no charity, and no tolerance, we shall never settle our differences amicably and must therefore always submit to the arbitration of a third party." Many of today's conflict management techniques and resolution process have a clear shadow of what and how Gandhi had seen inter-national issues in his times. A war-hunger nation has nothing in this world whilst a starving nation needs every kind of help from the world. A nation endangering peace in the world has no security for itself. He believed that peace can be achieve through a multi-dimensional and global efforts.

Martin Luther King Jr. is internationally recognized as the father of the civil rights movement. His nonviolent peaceful demonstrations proved to the world that action without violence can be effective and successful. He left a legacy of racial unity between whites and blacks. It is no longer legal in the United States to segregate or discriminate against anyone because of his or her skin color.

Former US President Donald Trump, during his four years in office, constantly emphasized diplomacy as a way of solving international conflicts. A typical example took place on December 19, 2019, at a NATO summit in London. Donald Trump declared that "we have peace" with North Korea and that he had a better "personal relationship" with Kim Jong Un. His statement was a great diplomatic message that favored peace rather than war. Despite human weaknesses, Trump will be remembered internationally as one of the American presidents who favored peaceful conflict resolution through diplomacy over going to war. He favored dialogue and mediation rather than military intervention. This was a good sign for a Christian leader, for the Bible says, "Peacemakers will be called the children of God" (Matthew 5:9).

God has blessed us with another peace-loving Christian leader who will lead this great country for another four years. The United States of America is currently at the center of the world. The entire world is looking to the United States for direction and exemplary leadership. We pray and believe that the new US leader will contribute to spreading hope by providing direction, policies, and actions that will contribute to the promotion and respect of human life, restoration of human dignity, and sustainable peace around the world. This will help in addressing the plight of refugees by bringing peace to war-affected countries. In the end, the most vulnerable refugees and asylum seekers living in refugee camps in many African countries and around the world may be safe to return to their home countries with dignity and to avail themselves of their national protection.

Conclusion

This chapter focused on the search for peace through diplomacy. It has appealed to our leaders around the world, believers, and all the people to participate in the search for world peace through dialogue, negotiation, mediation, and genuine political willingness and commitment. The emphasize was on brainstorming and the use of theories and practices that favor peaceful conflict resolution and transformation. Models such as Boutros Boutros-Ghali' "An Agenda for Peace: Preventive Diplomacy, Peacemaking, and Peacekeeping" were discussed.

The chapter also discussed the multitrack diplomacy approach to peace processes. True believers should promote peace through diplomacy and genuine political willingness to end war. There is no development without peace and no peace without development. Therefore, initiatives to build sustainable peace and security need to move hand in hand with economic development initiatives (north-south cooperation) that are mutually beneficial. The rule of law needs to be observed. Believers, especially those in leadership, need to play a leading role in the promotion of respect for human life and restoration of human dignity around the world. God is so pleased with us when we respect human life because we are created in His image. Therefore, we are more valuable than any other resource on earth. As the preacher said in the book of Ecclesiastes, all these other resources such as money and material things are "vanity of vanities. All is vanity" (Ecclesiastes 1:2–4).

We are the salt of the earth and the light of the world (Matthew 5:13–16). Let us promote peace through dialogue, negotiations, mediation, and genuine political willingness. Peace enforcement through military intervention should be used as the last resort. With this mindset and action, we can all address the predicament of refugees in a sustainable manner.

Again, I am grateful to the US government for bringing me and my family to this great country through the US Refugee Resettlement Program. May God bless America. May God bless Africa and the world at large. May God continue to use us and our leaders for His pleasure, glory, and honor. May God bless us and extend our sphere of influence, protect us, and keep us from the evil in Jesus Christ's name. May the peace of God prevail in this country and the world at large. May we open our hearts and our hands to welcome more refugees and support them to achieve their American dreams.

REFERENCES

Badibanga, M. L. 2010. "Educational Opportunities for Refugee Women and Girls in Zimbabwe. A Case Study of Refugee Women and Girls of Democratic Republic of Congo." Harare: Master's dissertation in women's law, University of Zimbabwe.

Berg, L. B. 2001. *Qualitative Research Methods in Social Sciences.* Long Beach, CA: University of California Publication.

Bhattacherjee, A. 2012. *Social Science Research: Principles, Methods and Practices.* Florida: University of Florida Publication.

Boomenyo Joseph. 2014. "Educational Opportunities and Sustainable Livelihoods Coping strategies for Refugee Youth in Zimbabwe. A Case Study of Tongogara Refugee Camp." Master's dissertation, Institute of Peace, Leadership and Governance of Africa University.

Bowd, R. and Chikwanha, A. B. 2010. *Understanding Africa's Contemporary Conflicts: Origins, Challenges and Peace Building.* Addis Ababa: Africa Human Security Initiative Publication.

Brian, G. 2011. *International Refugee Law and the United Nations.* New York: UNHCR Publication.

Burton, J. 1990. *Conflict: Human Needs Theory.* London: Macmillan.

Burton, J. 1990. *Conflict: Resolution and Prevention.* New York: St. Martin's Press.

Castles, S. 2003. Towards a Sociology of Forced Migration and Social Transformation. *Sociology* 31, no. 1: 13–34.

Chambers, R. 1995. "Poverty and Livelihoods: Whose Reality Counts?" ID discussion paper, 347 Brighton: IDS.

Christie, Daniel J. 1997. "Reducing Direct and Structural Violence: The Human Needs Theory." *Peace and Conflict: Journal of Peace Psychology* 3, no. 4.

Denzin, N., and Lincoln, Y., eds. 2005. *Handbook of qualitative research*. Third edition, Thousand Oaks, CA: Sage Publications.

Donnelly, J. 1998. *International Human Rights*. Second Edition. Boulder, CO: West-view Press.

Elespth, G and Violata, M. 2013. "CEPS in Liberty and Security: Current Challenges Regarding the International Refugee Law, with focus on EU Policies and EU Cooperation with UNHCR." CEPS (website). http://www.ceps.eu.

Everatt, D. 2010. *South Africans Civil Society and Xenophobia: A Synthesis*. Johannesburg: The Atlantic Philanthropies Publication.

Fullerton, M. 2011. *The Refugee Law Reader: Cases, Documents and Materials*. Sixth Edition, New York: Published by Hungarian Helsinki Committee, Budapest.

Given, L. M. 2008. *The SAGE Encyclopedia of Qualitative Research Methods*. 2 vols. Los Angeles: A SAGE Reference Publication.

Government of Zimbabwe. 2013. Constitution of Zimbabwe. Amendment (N0:20). Harare: Government Printers.

Government of Zimbabwe. 1983. Refugee Act Chapter 4:03. Harare: Government Printers.

Government of Zimbabwe. 2001. Zimbabwe Education Act Chapter 25:04. Harare: Government Printers.

Hathaway, J. C. 2007. "Why Refugee Law Still Matters." Melbourne: Melbourne Journal of International Law Publications.

Hattrell, F. 2010. "Redefining the Limits of Refugee Protection? The Securitised Asylum Policies of the 'Common European Asylum System.'" Master's thesis in European studies, University of Canterbury. Upper Richardton: National Centre for Research on Europe University of Canterbury Publication.

The Herald. 2014. "Backdated Pay for Civil Servants." "Least-Paid Worker to get $500" "Resources Mobilised, Govt Confirms." *The Herald* (Harare), April 9, 2014, 1.

Heyns, C. and Stefiszyn, K. 2006. *Human Rights, Peace and Justice in Africa*. Pretoria: Pretoria University Law Press.

Jinadu, L. A. 2007. "Explaining & Managing Ethnic Conflict in Africa: Towards a Cultural Theory of Democracy." Claude Ake Memorial Papers

No. 1, Department of Peace and Conflict Research Uppsala University & Nordic Africa Institute. Uppsala: Universitetstryckeriet Publication.

Kreuger, R. A. and Casey, M. A. 2000. *Focus Groups: A Practical Guide for Applied Research*. Third edition, Thousand Oaks, CA: Sage.

Mack, N., C. WoodSong, K. M. Macqueen, G. Guest, and E. Namey. 2011. *Qualitative Research Methods: A Data Collector's Field Guide*. North Carolina: Family Health International Publication.

Maslow, A. H. 1970. *Motivation and Personality*. New York: Harper and Row.

Maslow. A. H. 1943. *A Theory of Human Motivation*. Toronto: York University Publication.

McAdam, Jane. 2007. *Complementary Protection in International Refugee Law*. London: Oxford online Scholarship Publications.

Milner, J. 2011. *New Issues in Refugee Research: Refugee and Peace Building Process*. Ottawa: Carlton University Publication.

National Bioethics Advisory Commission. 2001. *Ethical and Policy Issues in Research Involving Human Participants*. Vol. 1, Report and Recommendations of the National Bioethics Advisory Commission. Maryland: NBAC Publication.

Peterson S. D. 2011. *Refugee Education, A Global Review*. Toronto: University of Toronto Publication.

Raftopoulos, B. and A. Mlambo. 2009. *Becoming Zimbabwe: A History from Precolonial Period to 2008*. Harare: Weaver Press.

Refugee Review Tribunal and Migration Review Tribunal. 2013. *A Guide to Refugee Law in Australia*. Sidney: Commonwealth of Australia Publications.

Ritchie, J. and J. Lewis. 2003. *Qualitative Research Practice: A Guide for Social Science Students and Researchers*. Thousand Oaks, CA: Sage Publications.

Steward, J. 1997. *Paving a Way Forward: A Review and Research Prime of WLSA Research Methodologies*. Harare: Women and Law in Southern Africa Research Project.

Stoner, J. A. F. 2006. *Management*. Sixth edition, New Delhi: Prentice Hall of India Publication.

The New York Bible Society. 2002. The New International Version Study Bible. Michigan: Zondervan Publication.

UNHCR. 1992. *Handbook on Procedures and Criteria for Determining Refugee Status under the 1951 Convention and the 1967 Protocol Relating to the Status of Refugees*. Geneva: UNHCR Publication.

UNHCR. 2005. *Refugee Protection: A Guide to International Refugee Law*. Geneva: UNHCR Publication.

United Nations Human Rights. 2008. *Claiming the Millennium Development Goals: A Human Rights Approach*. New York and Geneva: United Nations Publication.

University of Minnesota Centre for Bioethics. 2003. *A Guide to Research Ethics*. Minnesota: University of Minnesota Publication.

US Department of State, US Department of Homeland Security, US Department of Health and Human Services. 2020. *Proposed Refugee Admission for Fiscal Year 2021*. Report to Congress. Submitted on behalf of the President of the United States to the committees in the Judiciary United States Senate and United States House of Representatives in fulfillment of the requirements of section 207 (d) (1) and (e) of the Immigration and Nationality Act. US government official document available on the US Department of State website.

Suffolk University. 2012. *Conflict Minerals in the Congo: Blood Minerals and Africa's Under-Reported First World War*. Working Paper. Published in the United States.

Internet Resources

African Union. History of African Union. Accessed January 6, 2021. https://au.int/en/overview.

Ashishakiye, V., M. G. Bwoyero, and R. Nizigama. 2013. Our Voices: Conflict, Displacement and Land. Accessed February 17, 2014. http://www.opendemocracy.net/opensecurity/valerie-ashishakiye-marie-gorettibwoyero-rosette-nizigama/our-voices-conflict-displace/.

Australian Government. 2010. "Economic, Civic and Social Contributions of Refugees and Humanitarian Entrants: Literature Review Refugee Council of Australia." Accessed February 21, 2014. https://www.immi.gov.au/media/publications/research/_pdf/economic-civic socialcontributions-refugees-humanitarian-entrants-literature-review.pdf/.

Concern International. 2019.Accessed January 29, 2014. http://www. hkrac.org/wp-content/uploads/2013/10/Refugee-Concern-Network-Briefingto-Social-Welfare-Department-October-2021.pdf/.

D. Martin and K. Joomis.2007. Building Teachers: A Constructivist Approach to Introducing Education, "Maslow Hierarchy of Needs." Accessed January 20, 2021. http://www.cengage.com/resource uploads/downloads/0495570540 162121.pdf/.

Danielson, G. 2005. "Meeting Human Needs, Preventing Violence: Applying Human Needs Theory to the Conflict in Sri Lanka." Accessed March 20, 2014. www.humanneeds.org/srilanka.net/.

Em Griffin. "Hierarchy of Needs of Abraham Maslow." Accessed January 20, 2014. http://www.afirstlook.com/docs/hierarchy.pdf/.

Harding, J. and S. Varadan. 2010. "A Community-Based Approach to Refugee Protection in a Protracted Refugee Situation." Accessed February 22, 2014. http://www.odihpn.org/humanitarianexchange-magazine/ issue-46/a-community-based-approach-to-refugee-protection-in-aprotracted-refugee-situation/.

Hellen Bach, D. 2010. "Refugee Rights: Ethics, Advocacy and Africa." Accessed March 12, 2014. http://books.google.co.zw/books?id= PIvUl8TLOE4C&pg=PA68&dq=Refugee+encamp ment+model&hl= en&sa=X&ei=OPsJU7udK6mp0QWbzoHICw&ved=0CDEQuw UwAQ#v=onepage&q=Refugee%20encampment%20model&f=false'.

International Alert. What is Peacebuilding? Accessed January 6, 2021. https:// www.international-alert.org/what-we-do/what-is-peacebuilding?gclid=EAI aIQobChMIps_TkJqJ7gIVApSzCh0TQw8zEAAYAiAAEgJsxPD_BwE/

International Catholic Migration Commission. 2020. Accessed November 18, 2020. https://www.icmc.net/2020/11/18/forty-years-on-why-the-u-s-should-continue-to-welcome-refugees/.

Jonsson, U. 2010. "Human Rights Approach to Development Programming." Accessed February 20, 2014. http://www.unicef.org/rightsresults/ files/HRBDP Urban Jonsson April 2003.pdf/

Konyndk, J. 2010. "Towards a New Model for Post-Emergency Refugee Assistance." Accessed February 23, 2014. http://www.odihpn.org/ humanitarian-exchange-magazine/issue-31/towardsa-new-model-for-post-emergency-refugee-assistance/.

Marczak, M. and M. Sewell. 2010. "Using Focus Group for Evaluation."
Accessed January 27, 2014. http://ag.arizona.edu/sfcs/cyfernet/cyfar/
focus.htm/.

MONUSCO .2020, United Nations Peacekeeping Mission to the
DRC. Accessed in June 2021 https://en.wikipedia.org/wiki/
MONUSCO#:~:text=On%2025%20April%202006%2C%20
the,began%20on%2030%20July%202006/

Moy round, C. and J. and Katunga. 2006. "Coltan Exploration in Eastern
Democratic Republic of Congo (DRC)." Accessed March 1, 2014.
http://www.issafrica.org/pubs/Books/ScarcitySurfeit/Chapter4.pdf/.

Organization for African Unity. 1969. OAU Convention Governing the
Specific Aspects of Refugee Problems in Africa. Adopted on September
10, 1969, by the Assembly of Heads of State and Government. CAB/
LEG/24.3. It entered into force on June 20, 1974. http://www.achpr.org/
files/instruments/refugee-convention/achpr_instr_conv_refug_eng.pdf.

Parson, R. 2013. *Assessing the Economic Contributions of Refugees in Australia.
A Review of Literature.* Accessed February 20, 2014. http://www.mdainc.
org.au/sites/default/files/Assessing-the-economic-contribution-
ofrefugees-in-Australia-Final.pdf/.

Posner, M., and D. Clancy. 2013. "A Human Rights-Based Approach to
Refugee Assistance." Accessed March 12, 2021. http://www.cihc.org/
members/resource_library_pdfs/2_Law_and_Protection/2_6_
Rights based Assistance/HR Based approach to Refugee Assistance.pdf/.

Refugee Consortium of Kenya. 2013. "Refugee Management in Kenya."
Accessed February 23, 2014. http://www.fmreview.org/FMRpdfs/
FMR16/fmr16.6.pdf/.

Refugee Law Initiative. 2012. "Rights Displaced: The Effects of Long-Term
Encampment on the Human Rights of Refugees." Working Paper No 4.
Accessed February 17, 2014. http://sas-space.sas.ac.uk/4691/1/RLI_
Working_Paper_No.4.pdf/.

Relief International (2020) Humanitarian Situation in the Democratic
Republic of Congo http://reliefweb.int/sites/reliefweb.int/files/
resources/Full Document 20.pdf/.

Sage. 2019. Ethical Issues in Conducting Research. Accessed January
22,2020 https://www.sagepub.com/sites/default/files/upm-
binaries/4999_Polonski_Chapter_5.pdf

Transend Media Service. 2020. The Wisdom of Johan Galtung, Father of Peace and Conflict Studies. Accessed February 2021. https://www.transcend.org/tms/2020/12/the-wisdom-of-johan-galtung-father-of-peace-and-conflict-studies/

Schmidt, A. 2012. "FMO Thematic Guide: Camps Versus Settlements." Accessed February 23, 2014. http://www.forcedmigration.org/research-resources/expert-guides/camps versus settlements/fmo021.pdf/.

Southern Eye. 2014. "Fresh Waves of Zim Migrants Flee Worsening Economy." April 26, 2014. Accessed April 26, 2014. http://www.southerneye.co.zw/2014/03/23/fresh-waves-zim-migrants-fleeworsening-economy/.

Southern Eye (2014). "Cost of Living Increases." April 20, 2014. Accessed April 27, 2014. www.southerneye.co.zw/2014/01/03/cost-of-living-increases/.

The League of Nations. 1920–1946. Accessed February 17, 2014. http://geography.about.com/od/politicalgeography/a/The-League-Of-Nations.htm/.

UNHCR. 2014. "Statistics and Facts about Asylum Seeker and Refugee Issues." http://www.unhcr.org/pages/49c3646c1d.html/ on 10 March 2014.

UNHCR. 2013. "UNHCR Mid-Year Trends 2013." Accessed March 2, 2014. http://www.unhcr.org/52af08d26.html/. Accessed January 21, 2021

United States Institute of Peace. 2012. "Return and Resettlement of Refugees and Internally Displaced Peoples." Accessed January 22, 2014. http://www.usip.org/guiding-principlesstabilization-and-reconstruction-the-web-version/10-social-well-being/return-and/.

University of Colorado. 2012. *The Beyond Intractability Project: The Conflict Information Consortium.* Accessed January 10, 2014. http://www.beyondintractability.org/m/huma needs.jps/.US Government.179. Bill of Rights. US Constitution. https://www.law.cornell.edu/constitution/billofrights/ accessed in February 2021.

UNESCO. 2004. UNESCO Constitution. Accessed February 20, 2014. http://portal.unesco.org/en/ev.phphtml/.

UNHCR. 2012. "Global Trends 2012 in Review: Trends at a Glance." Accessed March 1, 2019. http://unhcr.org/globaltrendsjune2013/UNHCR%20GLOBAL%20TRENDS%202012_V05.pdf/.

UNHCR. 2006. "Refugee Livelihood: A Review of the Evidence." Accessed February 15, 2014. http://www.unhcr.org/4423fe5d2.pdf/.

UNHCR. 2006. "Human Rights and Refugee Protection. Self-Study Module 5, Vol 2." Accessed January 29, 2014. http://www.refworld.org/pdfid/4669434c2.pdf/accessed.

UNHCR. 2014. "2014 Country Operation Profiles—Kenya." Accessed February 28, 2014. http://www.unhcr.org/pages/49e483a16.html/.

UNHCR 2014. "2014 UNHCR Operation Profile—Southern Africa." Accessed April 27, 2014. http://www.unhcr.org/pages/49e4856b6.html/.

United Nations. "Governance." Accessed February 24, 2014. http://www.un.org/en/globalissues/governance/.

UNESCO (2015) Building Peace in the minds of men and women. http://www.unesco.org/new/unesco/about-us/who-we-are/history/constitution/ Accessed November 2021

UNHCR (2015) Refugee Encampment Policy. www.refugee-encampment.com/ accessed June 2021

United Nations.2018. Definition of Youth. Accessed February 5, 2021. https://www.un.org/esa/socdev/documents/youth/fact-sheets/youth-definition.pdf /.

United States Government. Definition of Youth/Accessed February 5, 2021. https://www.youthpolicy.org/factsheets/country/united-states/. Accessed February 5, 2021. https://allafrica.com/stories/202011110506.html.

NYU Education. 2007. What is Research Design? Accessed March 11, 2014. http://www.nyu.edu/classes/bkg/methods/005847ch1.pdf/.

Human Rights Watch. .2020. World Report: The Democratic Republic of Congo, Events of 2019. Accessed January 6, 2021. https://www.hrw.org/world-report/2020/country-chapters/democratic-republic-congo/

Accessed January 10, 2021. https://en.wikipedia.org/wiki/Imperialism/.

Worldmeters.2021. Zimbabwe Population. Accessed January 28, 2021. https://www.worldometers.info/world-population/zimbabwe-population/#:~:text=Zimbabwe%202020%20population%20is%20estimated,of%20the%20total%20world%20population.

Accessed January 28, 2021. https://www.theafricareport.com/57779/zimbabwe-lockdown-amid-covid-surge-has-no-support-for-people/.

Tel sure. 2020. Libya: Before and After Muammar Gaddafi/ Accessed January 30, 2021. https://www.telesurenglish.net/analysis/Libya-Before-and-After-Muammar-Gaddafi-20200115-0011.html.

Accessed February 8, 2021. https://www.theguardian.com/us-news/2021/feb/08/covid-19-variants-deaths-us-tracking.

Accessed February 14, 2021. https://www.wrapsnet.org/admissions-and-arrivals/.

Accessed February 16, 2021. https://www.un.org/en/sc/repertoire/8992/Chapter%208/GENERAL%20ISSUES/Item%2029_Agenda%20for%20peace_.pdf.

Accessed February 16, 2021. https://www.theatlantic.com/politics/archive/2019/12/donald-trump-kim-jong-un-north-korea-diplomacy-denuclearization/603748/.

Accessed February 20, 2021. https://www.worldometers.info/world-population/us-population/.

Accessed February 22, 2021. https://www.unhcr.org/ke/figures-at-a-glance.

Accessed March 11, 2021. https://www.galtung-institut.de/en/home/johan-galtung/.

Accessed March 11, 2021. https://www.irenees.net/bdf_fiche-notions-186_en.html.

Accessed March 11, 2021. https://castle.eiu.edu/~wow/classes/fa03/mlkcontributions.htm.

Accessed March 11, 2021. https://www.mkgandhi.org/articles/gandhiworldofpeace.html.

Printed in the United States
by Baker & Taylor Publisher Services